LOST ON THE WAY

LOST ON THE WAY

A Journal From the Camino de Santiago

BLAKE FARHA

ISBN Paperback: 978-1-7363946-2-5
ISBN Electronic: 978-1-7363946-0-1
ISBN Audio: 978-1-7363946-1-8

Disclaimer: I have tried to recreate events, locales and conversations from my memories of them. To protect privacy, I have changed the names of individuals and places, and I have changed some identifying characteristics and details such as physical properties, occupations and places of residence. The events recorded in this book are those I remember to the best of my ability, though others may have a different take on these events. No harm or injury is intended by anything recorded in this book.

The information provided in this book is for general information about health. This book is not intended as medical or health advice, nor is considered a substitute for professional medical expertise or treatment. If you have any concerns about your physical or mental health, please be sure to consult with your medical professional.

The author is not responsible for any health issues, advice, or guidance provided in the book, nor is liable for any physical, psychological, emotional, or health damages. The use of the information provided in this book is solely at your own risk. You are responsible for your own actions and decisions.

www.BlakeFarha.com

Dedicated to anyone who was ever lost
and in need of a bit of companionship.

Contents

LOST ON THE WAY

Foreword

As author of my own international bestselling Camino memoir, *The Only Way Is West*, I was humbled and honoured when Blake, a fellow author, writer and podcaster, asked me to write the foreword for this book.

Blake and I first connected when I interviewed him for an episode of my podcast, *El Camino de Santiago Pilgrims' Podcast*.

What struck me immediately about him, as he retold the before, during and after story of his pilgrimage, was his bravery to gain a better understanding of his mental health struggles; his honesty about those successes and failures as well as his resulting vulnerability. The interview was unfiltered, deeply revealing and candid, just like this book.

What also shone throughout our conversation, was his love for the Camino and gratitude for it giving him time and space; a platform to grow and evolve through his personal challenges; a stage for personal healing to take place.

Lost On the Way is a must read for anyone looking for a real life tale about the Camino, not a fairy tale. It documents in great detail the extreme highs and lows; the good, the bad and the ugly injuries and blisters a pilgrim may have to endure on the way to Santiago.

It's also for anyone wondering how walking the Camino de Santiago can aid a person to get the upper-hand and stay one step ahead of their own mental health demons. You'll find some simple, yet effective strategies and techniques that have helped Blake and can help you, too.

An enchanting example is how he records three things he's grateful for and proud of at the end of each day. Like me, you're probably going to want to put an arm around him as you read. You're going to be rooting for him all the way.

I was proud of Blake reading these lines towards the end of his journey: "Blake was the glue that held our Camino family together - to Blake!" a member of his adopted Camino family says, raising a glass.

People were being kind to Blake because he'd finally learned how to be kind to himself.

It's a reminder of something we should all do for ourselves more often and one of many poignant reflections and powerful lessons you'll find between the covers of *Lost On the Way*.

¡Buen Camino fellow peregrinos!

Bradley Chermside
Author of *The Only Way Is West.*

Preface

Hitting the Road

I was fuming. An icy mixture of confusion, terror, and fury swirled together, swept through my body, and crept into every appendage before morphing into a general physical numbness in stark contrast with the tempest of outrage exploding in my brain. My fluorescent lines of code, succinctly stacked in neat, carefully indented rows filling the computer screen at which I stared blankly, began melting into a language I was suddenly incapable of comprehending, let alone working with.

Staring out across the river Spree, my boss informed me quietly, regrettably that my name was on the long list of people who would be laid off in the coming days from the startup in which I had worked for over three-and-a-half-years.

Now, seated at my desk, the usual din of the open office faded into a mere hum in the background. The unsettled clamor of colleagues and coworkers whirring around me, many of whom their heads, unbeknownst to them, already lay on the proverbial chopping block. All their overt preoccupations with innovating, disrupting, and failing faster seemed at once so futile, so pointless, so utterly without purpose. As the initial shock of the news subsided, only two thoughts were left burning in my head.

The first, an indignant, incredulous, perhaps self-important, "Me? Me?! They're laying *me* off?! After everything I've given and done for this company? This is the thanks I get for the years of dedication and hard work?"

The second, more flippant than belligerent, "Screw it, then. I'm walking the Camino."

The Call of The Camino

My affair with the Camino started in 2011 when my teaching contract in France was nearing its end and I found myself in a time of uncertainty. A colleague suggested walking the Camino might help me find some clarity. The thought of spending thirty days traipsing across the Spanish countryside from the Pyrenees clear to the Atlantic Ocean, accompanied by thousands of other souls on a mission, immediately appealed to me. In the five years between when I first heard about the Camino and that fateful day in 2017 when I learned I would soon find myself unwillingly and, in my mind, unjustly unemployed, the call of the Camino rang like the tinnitus in my ears - sometimes altogether unnoticeable amidst the ruckus of other distractions, occasionally overwhelming enough to keep me from sleeping, but constantly present. From the outset I knew that if I wanted to quiet it's dogged pleas for my attention, I had but one option: pack a bag and get underway.

Suddenly, the impediment of a full time job was no longer an excuse, and I found myself with no clear goals, obligations, or benchmarks in the foreseeable future. After five years and a couple of half-earnest flirtations with setting off on the age-old pilgrimage, the time had finally come.

A few weeks after I left my office for the last time, I haphazardly booked a one-way flight to Paris and a bus to Saint-Jean Port de Pied, the small city at the foot of the Pyrenees where the most traveled Camino begins. I began preparing for the trip with three things on my mind: adventure, perspective, and mental stability.

More than anything, the journey across Spain appealed to the extroverted outdoorsman bursting with wanderlust in me. From those first camping trips my family took to nearby lakes in the woodlands of northern Texas, I always loved the outdoors. Over the years I began to dabble in hiking, hitting a trail whenever the opportunity presented itself, and slowly gathered more and more experience. From the Mexican Hill Country around Guanajuato to the open plains in central France to the modest mountains all over South Korea, I came to find the challenge of a strenuous hike as intoxicating as the chance to connect a bit with nature. My heart raced every time I imagined myself on the Camino blazing along trails cut through forests, deserts, mountains, and tiny forgotten pueblos. My feet itched at the thought of spending all day every day in the marvelous Spanish countryside making new friends and gorging myself on regional Spanish delicacies along the way.

Apart from an excuse to spend an entire month basking in the invigorating Spanish sunshine, the Camino would give me time and space to think, which I hoped would lead to the discovery of a new path for myself. Suddenly jobless, the future lay before me like an open desert with no visible beacons, landmarks, or checkpoints at which to aim. I possessed no semblance of a road map, my only guide the knowledge that wherever I had come from was no longer an option. No, I couldn't go back to web development. Or startups. Or school. Nor could I go back to teaching English, managing a yogurt shop, working in finance, customer service, product ownership, recruitment, or even my life as a starving but striving singer-songwriter. None of those things would do. But eventually I'd have to eat. Eventually I'd have to convince the German bureaucrats at the immigration office that I amounted to an asset to the German State, deserving of a cherished and fiercely guarded work visa. With any luck the Camino would not only satisfy my craving for an exhilarating expedition, but it might help me plan the first few cautious steps into the uncharted territory that awaited me back in Berlin.

More than just a chance to answer the call of the wild, more than an escape for those in need of a bit of perspective, the Camino is first and foremost a spiritual journey, and it's fair to say that my spirit needed bolstering even more than I needed some time in the great outdoors, or a new career path.

To put it mildly, I've never been what most people would call a "happy" person. In fact, I was only twelve years old the first time I deeply considered killing myself. It's difficult for me to gauge the seriousness or efficacy of the schemes the juvenile version of myself concocted to take his own life, or what prevented him from seeing them through. But what's certain is those schemes and suicidal thoughts were silent harbingers of the crippling depression, anxiety, and hopelessness that would hound me for the rest of my life. Like so many who suffer from these insidious maladies, I possessed a shocking ignorance of the very ills that consumed me from the inside. The days spent paralyzed and sobbing, unable to get out of bed or off the floor; the crushing feelings of dread and the complete loss of appetite for anything, including foods, activities, and people that once brought me immense joy; the countless suicidal thoughts varying in degrees of detail, severity, and sincerity sometimes triggered by shockingly small problems. I had no idea these symptoms warned of something so much graver than my amateur self-diagnosis of just being a sensitive guy with a tendency to be a bit hard on himself.

Eventually, at the age of twenty-five, thanks to the insistence of my then girlfriend, it finally became clear to me that the pain and suffering with which I experienced my daily life was neither common, nor the experience of the vast majority of people. It finally became clear that I needed professional help. At the time I lost my job in 2017 I was already back in therapy for the second time and well on my way to a life unfettered by these lifelong frenemies. I intended to capitalize on the utterly simple life of a pilgrim to create the space necessary to solidify the new habits and mindsets my therapist and I had worked hard to build within me. I hoped that such prolonged exposure to the spirituality saturating the Camino would dispel the lingering hopelessness often responsible for thrusting me into that familiar downward spiral.

The Decision to Journal

Not long before I left for the Camino, I came across a book called "Happier" written by the positive psychologist and Harvard professor, Dr. Tal Ben-Shahar. The book, a must-read for anyone struggling with depression or interested in the subject of happiness, details many habits which have been shown to promote general well-being based on the latest scientific research. Of all the fascinating information I found in those pages, I was particularly struck by the research on journaling. According to Dr. Ben-Shahar, for those with a tendency to ruminate, it can be a powerful tool, not only for processing those nasty thoughts stuck on a loop in the brain, but also for finding solutions and coming to conclusions when answers refuse to manifest themselves in a busy mind.

I myself am no stranger to deep rumination. This destructive mental habit often catalyzes a long slide into the yawning abyss lurking at the bottom of my mind, and works to the detriment of both my mental health and my ability to live in and enjoy the moment. If I intended to get any serious, productive thinking done while on the Camino, a daily journal might act as a filter for effectively processing any thoughts on my past, present, or future which might arise over the course of the day. Writing down the goings-on in my head could possibly even prevent the intense brooding to which I'm extremely prone. In addition, a well-kept journal would act as a keepsake for what I hoped would constitute a formative journey full of tiny moments worth remembering. I knew if these were left undocumented, they would inevitably slip through the cracks in my mind to be lost among a sea of memories deemed unremarkable by my subconscious, and eventually flushed entirely out of my brain to make room for things of somehow greater consequence.

So, at the behest of my new happiness guru, I made space among the carefully selected and meticulously cataloged items in my spartanly packed rucksack for a single ballpoint pen and a small, cheap notebook which I swore to myself I would write in every day of the journey.

If I wanted this Camino journal to serve me well on my journey to self-improvement and mental clarity, I realized I would have to consciously work against any kind of self-editing or self-censorship. The reflections it would eventually contain could benefit me only as sincere and authentic representations of my experience of the world. Therefore, I would have to make a deliberate and concerted effort to record everything exactly as I recalled and lived it in as unbiased a manner as possible, even if what I wrote seemed inflammatory or unpopular. I would need to document everything I felt, thought, and perceived as honestly and accurately as possible; the good, and perhaps especially, the bad and the ugly. To the extent that I was able, being of course only a human subject to my own biases, fears, and imperfections, I kept this intention alive and present, willing it to preside over every single word written on the pages of this journal.

The Decision to Publish

If indeed I intended this document to serve only as a personal record of events and a private log of intimate reflections, how then has it come to exist in such a public form as a self-published book? After I completed the Camino and before I returned to Berlin, I spent two days in Coimbra, Portugal where I read the entirety of what I wrote throughout the journey that led me there. Holding the raggedy notebook in my hands and reading over my words was not only an extremely gratifying experience, it was also a rather enlightening one. Day by day, kilometer by kilometer, the Camino, the people I met, and the time I spent reflecting on the thoughts which punctuated the way bestowed lesson after lesson upon me which I eagerly inked onto the dog-eared pages. To my surprise, many of them had already slipped the grip of my long-term memory and I felt as though I were reading them for the first time.

At the risk of seeming self-aggrandizing, egotistical, and arrogant, I genuinely believed that these same insights could potentially serve others. Not long after finishing the last page, I felt a sudden urge to publish the journal I never meant to show anyone. I hoped that these lessons might resonate with and inform people who may never have the privilege of thirty-three unbroken days of introspection and inspiring encounters, as well as those who might and those who already have. I decided to publish this journal out of a sincere desire to help anyone who might be helped by it; who might somehow gain something, anything, from my experience; who might feel a sense of connection with another lost soul attempting to overcome his own demons and find his way in the desert of uncertainty, insecurity, and fear.

In an effort to publish my journal as honestly and with as much integrity as possible, I have transcribed it precisely, word for word, as I found it on the pages I wrote every day of the journey across Spain and beyond. Except for where I felt it necessary to protect the privacy and identities of the people I wrote about, I have left it unedited in every sense of the word. Not a single word has been altered from those battered pages tucked in a messy dresser drawer and held together by threads or altogether torn from the cheap metal wire to which they once clung. Therefore, the reader may notice occasional errors scattered throughout this book. Errors of spelling, grammar, and syntax have been painstakingly double-checked with the original journal and left as I originally wrote them, however wrong they may be. Some inconsistencies of time and place may crop up. There are no fewer than five different spellings of "Finisterre." I have left them all at the risk of confusing or annoying the reader, as I felt editing a single letter of the journal could create a slippery slope potentially leading to editing whole words, passages, or entire entries of the original document. So, any and all errors found within the journal are not errors of oversight or poor typing. They have been noted, checked, and intentionally left as they were mistakenly written. By leaving it untouched, I hope to preserve the integrity of the words I wrote as much as humanly possible. It's through their honesty that any real message, lesson, or insight might be transmitted; it's in their sincerity that any value, perceived or real, exists.

Exceptions and Clarifications

As mentioned, there are some caveats to the "no editing" rule, which I hope the reader will forgive, and which for the sake of openness and honesty I'll enumerate here.

1. Names, nationalities, and physical characteristics of every person mentioned in the journal have been changed in an effort to protect their privacy.

2. For the sake of consistency and clarity, the placement of the "Pride and Gratitude" section, which I will discuss momentarily, has been moved to the end of every journal entry, while in the original document I generally began each entry with it.

3. Nearly all mentions of measurement or weight of any kind were originally written in the metric system. For the sake of any reader unfamiliar with the metric system, I later added the corresponding equivalence in imperial units (feet, yards, miles, pounds, etc.) to any mention of measure or weight found throughout the journal.

4. Some journal entries included no mention of the time at which they were written, and in these instances I added "no time recorded" for the sake of consistency.

5. A single footnote was added to this journal in order to correct a factual error I made. Having discovered the mistake only after I returned from the Camino, I wanted to address it outright so as not to misinform the reader with the original false information.

6. Though it may go without saying, the original journal does not include any photos. I added the photos to the digital version of the journal later.

7. A few pages at the end of the journal which I used to track my overall progress across the Camino, as well as pages used for tracking my spending and monitoring my daily mental-health habits have been omitted, as I didn't feel they were pertinent to the overall goals of publishing this journal.

To the best of my knowledge, those are the only changes I have made to the original handwritten journal.

I took and edited all the photos displayed throughout *Lost on the Way*. Each of the photos has been placed in the journal to correspond to the respective section of the Camino on which they were originally taken. I hope they act as a visual aid to give readers a sense of the things I came across that motivated and inspired me throughout the journey. Admittedly, there are countless kilometers of dreary, unsightly, and downright hideous stretches of the Camino. Their omission from this journal is not to project a false sense that every moment of the journey is like walking through an exotic postcard. While the vast majority of the Camino transects gorgeous countrysides and quaint pueblos, I marched through plenty of unsightly landscapes, as I'll often mention throughout the journal. I simply didn't take the time to photograph those parts of the journey. I apologize to anyone interested in the less photo-worthy views I saw along the way.

At the end of nearly every entry is a section called "Pride and Gratitude." In 2016, at my therapist's request, I began a "pride and gratitude" journal in which every day I wrote down three things I did that made me feel proud and three things that happened for which I was grateful. These six sentences formed an integral part of my mental health toolbox, and I still log them every day almost without exception, and likely will for the rest of my life.

A Final Word

So there you have it. The ins and outs of how this journal came into existence, and all the reasons for which I wrote it, and eventually decided to publish it.

May this record of my time on The Camino de Santiago serve all who read it in some way. May it bring comfort to those who are lost, scared, uncertain, downtrodden or struggling with their own demons - physical, mental, or otherwise. May it impassion the adventurous and outdoorsy. May it inspire the unmotivated and the deflated. May it inform the introspective. May it incite a smile for those in need of humor and warm the hearts of those in need of connection. May it serve as a reminder that the road is life. May it awaken hope in all who read it because, contrary to what I've believed for nearly my entire life, there is always hope, and, if we know where to look for it, usually in great abundance.

Day -6

BERLIN, GERMANY

*A*nd so begins the first in a series of entries detailing my trip along the Camino Frances, a specific portion of the series of trails that lead to Santiago de Compostela, the final resting place of the Apostle, St. James the Greater.

I made the decision to take this trip...well, perhaps I should back up a bit.

I first heard about the Camino de Santiago at the age of 25, when I was living in France teaching English in a tiny city called Auxerre. That was 2012. I was nearing the end of my contract, and, having just broken up with my girlfriend at the time, Carolina, a Portuguese woman I had met in Spain while we were studying in Castellón, and who was the last living artifact of that very innocent, youthful time in 2009, I was very unsure of what to do next.

A teacher/friend of mine, who was half German, half French, suggested I consider doing El Camino and take some time to think about the next step. That was the first I ever heard of it, and I was captivated instantly.

Opting instead for a lightning, 6-week trip around Europe on a bus

before returning to Austin, Texas to chase my dreams of being a musician, I left the Camino for another time.

I would often think about El Camino when I was feeling fed up with my life and the direction it was taking. I took great solace in the thought of being on the road, the journey the only real goal, nothing to do all day but walk, think, and enjoy the stunning Spanish scenery.

When I finally decided I had had enough of Austin, my dreams, and the place that was supposed to be my home, I decided I would return to Europe to start over from scratch. That was in August of 2013. I planned to, first and foremost, quit playing music. I couldn't take another weeknight playing in a dingy bar to an audience so desensitized to live music that I may as well have been playing to an empty room for all the interaction I was capable of drawing out of the handful of people I had the pleasure of playing to.

I decided to take a 2nd part-time English teaching job to start socking away the money so I could return to Europe in May 2014. And I would start by walking El Camino.

I started doing research and reading up on it, and interrogating Carol, a musician living in Austin who had done El Camino twice already.

Then I met Patricia and decided that the Camino would have to wait.

Patricia moved back to Copenhagen in January of 2014, and I met her there in March. We lived there for two-and-a-half months before moving to Berlin together, where we thought it would be easier for me to get a visa and a job, which it most certainly was.

I began working for a very small, 5-month old startup called CareerFoundry as their 8th employee, and to make a long story very short, in May 2017 there was a round of layoffs which cut the 30-odd person team nearly in half, and my name was on the list.

The second thought that went through my head when my boss gave me the news, just after, "Are you serious? They're firing me?" was, "Maybe now's the time to walk El Camino."

And, after toying with the idea for a few weeks, I bought the plane → bus → train tickets to get to St. Jean Port-de-Pied, the city which marks the beginning of El Camino Frances in July.

Since then, I've been doing everything I can to prepare for my month-long, 800 KM journey across Spain.

I've been reading guide books, blogs, talking with friends of friends who have done it, and getting all my equipment.

I've been going on walks in my boots to break them in, and lotioning my feet everyday to make sure the skin is soft and elastic to help prevent blistering.

I packed my bag with everything I'll be taking last week and have been taking it with me on practice runs around the city to try to make adjustments before I start.

Today I took a <u>very long</u> practice run, walking for four hours with my full pack for a distance of approximately 17.1 KM (10.6 mi.)

According to the guides I've been reading, a pilgrim should complete approximately 25 KM (15 mi.) per day to finish the trail in a month, which should usually take five to six hours.

This may seem like a lot of preparation. I doubt many pilgrims go to such lengths before they embark on their journey. But I feel I must. I feel I must because...I'm scared. I'm scared that I can't do it. I'm scared I won't be able to make it to Santiago de Compostela. And I think after today, I'm more scared than I was before. In fact, the thought of the first day brings tears to my eyes. I'm really scared.

I have been trying to prepare for this journey as much as I possibly could because I'm terrified of failing, and I hoped that by preparing so much, I'd give myself the greatest chance of "success," by which I mean: walking all the way to Santiago de Compostela. And one of the things today's practice run taught me was this: No amount of preparation is going to prevent this journey from being very difficult.

In my head it didn't seem like it would be that tough, even when I thought of all the potential difficulties.

The Heat of August - pff...I'm from Texas. Bring the heat!

The Walking! - pff...I'm 30, cycle all over Berlin, march all over cities all across the world, and workout three times per week. I'm in the best shape of my life. I hike up and down mountains and all over parks and countryside without stopping, complaining, or blistering. Bring it.

The Loneliness! - I've always traveled alone, and have been pretty far all by myself. No problem.

But an hour into my walk today, my feet were not feeling well. I decided to buy nice boots for the trip, even though I only ever wear sneakers. Sneakers have taken me all over the world and I've never gotten a blister that I can recall. These boots, however, as much as I've tried to break them in, it seems are simply too small.

I took them off halfway through my trip today, stuffed them in my bag, and walked the rest of the way in an old pair of flip flops I bought in Croatia in 2012. My feet were much happier, and I managed to avoid blistering.

Currently, my feet are my biggest concern. I bought the boots (German made, German Quality, 100% waterproof, contragrip 4 inches thick, made especially for trekking and mountaineering) thinking they would be my best line of defence against the terrain. But it seems my unfamiliarity with boots led me astray in terms of how to size them and break them in. They're too tight on the toes, though otherwise super comfy and super sturdy. Bt they threaten to rub my pinky toes raw. It seems I may have no choice but to tackle El Camino in the same black Nike's that got me through a 9 hour hike up to 3,500 meters of Mt. Kazbeg and back without a single blister, and only a few tumbles.

So, I'm scared. I'm scared that all my preparation has been as useless as my attempt at buying appropriate footwear.

I, eternally a perfectionist with a huge chip on my shoulder, am afraid I'll fail at this mission of mine.

Still, this is precisely why I've done so much preparation: to learn and improve before I begin. It seems it would be prudent, then, to consider what my walk today taught me.

1. This will be tough, no matter how much you prepare. And that is okay. In fact, it's probably part of the point.
2. So much walking is lovely, and very meditative.
3. My pack is plenty light, and didn't prove too troublesome.
4. My boots, which I bought a size too big, are either not broken in enough, too small, or both.
5. My flip-flops are still in great shape, and can definitely get me around if need be.
6. Four hours flies by when walking.
7. My pack isn't too heavy, but it may cause friction burns on my hips if I'm not careful.
8. It's better to rest briefly, frequently, than to rest once for a while.
9. Walking to the rhythm of "Stayin' Alive," which is 100 beats

per minute equals 100 steps per minute, and seems to be a good pace.

10. I need a hat.

11. I will have to be vigilant, as alone time can easily lead me to dark places in my head. I'll have to have all my tools at the ready to keep me mentally strong.

12. Listen to your feet. Really. Listen.

13. A little gauze and a bit of sports tape go a long way in terms of aching toes.

14. Keep the first aid kit in the most easily reachable part of the backpack.

15. I'm in great shape! I could definitely have kept walking another few hours, and was never really winded or tired.

16. Don't forget: this will be tough. But it's supposed to be.

Tomorrow I'll unpack my bag, go over my checklist once again, make sure I've got everything, then re-pack it.

Then I think I'll write a bit about why I'm doing this in the first place, and what I might like to get out of it.

All my lovin',

- Blake.

Day -5

BERLIN, GERMANY

Today I have managed to rekindle excitement about my trip. What had become a mixture of stress and fear has been warped into a sense of excitement and readiness.

I gave up on the shoes I had originally bought for the trip. They were <u>too small</u> and, after asking a handful of friends who are avid hikers or have actually done parts of the trail what they thought about my predicament, I decided to get rid of them. The general consensus was, "Go with what your feet know."

I was fortunate to have the chance to speak with Jared, a friend and avid hiker who has scaled major peaks in over 20 countries. He gave me some excellent advice, and with it I went this morning to buy a pair of the ugliest, orangest, lightest, most comfortable pair of shoes I've ever owned. He assured me they are made for tough terrains, but are light and made for running on trails, and will be more than adequate for the Camino.

I've walked in them all day without issue, apart from the unceasing looks they are attracting from aghast passersby, who clearly can't believe anyone would be so bold as to break the Berlin Black rule so flagrantly.

So, my biggest fear about this trip, having adequate footwear for my only mode of transport on the trail has, at least for now, been assuaged!

Next: My fear of the hordes of people on the "Camino Frances." Currently, over 50,000 people are on that trail during the month of August. The albergues along the route house between 100 and 200 people at a time. Getting a bed means getting up early, and trying to beat the crowds of people there. I've been very worried about this.

Today, I decided at the behest of Carol, a friend and musician from Austin who has walked the Camino Frances twice. After giving some advice on the footwear issue, she changed gears to outright begging me to reconsider my choice of path. She claims in August that the trail becomes a veritable Disneyland, flooded with so many people as to render the solitude of the journey all but nonexistent.

I have decided to forgo the Camino Frances for the Camino Del Norte ("North Road"). Situated about 82 KM (51 mi.) to the north of El Camino Frances, El Camino Del Norte runs along the Spanish coast, sandwiched between the Cantabrian Mountains to the South, and the Bay of Biscay to the North. While the scenes are meant to be breathtaking, including idyllic deserted beaches, and green forests blowing in the ocean breeze, it's hilliness is quite intimidating to most, and it's pilgrim infrastructure not being quite as abundant as on El Camino Frances scare the majority of people from embarking upon it.

That said, the infrastructure is still excellent and it should be far less busy than El Camino Frances. So, I will embark instead upon this lesser travelled road, thus alleviating fear number two.

So, now there is nothing left to do but find a guide, and get going!

Day -5

Today I unpacked my bag, double-checked my checklist, and repacked. I'm as ready as I'm going to be, and it feels good to be excited about it again.

All my lovin',

- Blake.

Day -2

PARIS, FRANCE

Saturday, August 19th, 2017

no time recorded

*W*here yesterday ended and today began is difficult to define. Yesterday was an incredibly busy day spent visiting lawyers to discuss my visa, saying goodbye to friends all over the city, putting the final touches on my packing, calling family to say goodbye, baking a cake for Boss Life, having our first Boss Life meeting, and finding time to catch up on the news as well. Miraculously, there was no last minute panic, which is probably entirely due to the fact that I was too busy to panic.

I finally got into bed at 1:00 AM, my alarm set for 4:00 AM, and between the incredible amount of noise taking place in the Berlin streets at that hour (noise which has never beforehand bothered me because I tend to be among those making the noise), and the fear that I might sleep through my alarm, I was kept in a constant state of semi-consciousness.

When I left the house at 4:15, it was with a heavy heart, and even heavier eyelids.

I was fortunate to have had the calmest, quietest flight in history, (and the window seat, to boot!) so I managed to get a little sleep on the plane. Arriving at 9:5 AM, my bus not leaving until 22:15, I had a whole day to kill, and thought about getting some sleep in the safety of the airport.

However, the weather was magnificent, cool and sunny, with a hint of the coming Autumn kissing the trees and occasionally filling the wafting breeze, so I decided to suck it up and make a day out of it, and what a day it <u>was</u>!

I have always loved Paris. I don't know if it's because of the image the world has built into it, or if it is contaminated with the nostalgia of my first trip to Paris, where I spent four days with three of my best friends and a beautiful woman I was in love with, but there is a magical and powerful nostalgia that fills my heart every time I grace the streets of this deceptively romantic city.

I say deceptively romantic because it brandishes all the markings of a major metropolitan area: blatant poverty, homelessness and inequality, noise, pollution, rubbish, and a general weighty brusqueness, and yet, in spite of all that, there is something slightly magical in the air.

I headed straight for Montmartre, home to a bakery with allegedly the best croissants in the city, the incredible Cathedral, Sacre Cœur, and some of my fondest memories of Paris.

I enjoyed the delicious croissant, and a Paris Brest, my favorite French pastry, perched atop the hill of the Sacre Cœur, smiling constantly as I pictured Juan, Jonas, Stefano, Alyssa, Carolina and myself making a picnic on the steps of our first site in Paris.

Walking around the streets of Montmartre, I was filled with a sense of joy and nostalgia and couldn't help but find it very fitting that what is perhaps my greatest adventure to date begins where my first great adventure ended.

Paris was our last stop on our Road Trip, 19 days of driving, camping in bushes, site seeing, partying, non-stop laughter, and more chopped pork sandwiches than anyone should be forced to consume. We were living in luxury in Paris with a kitchen and actual beds to sleep in. I was spending my nights in a hotel with Carolina. It was fantastic.

So as I traipsed all over the city, finally visiting the cafe from one of my favorite films, Amelie, and spending most of my afternoon wandering through Le Parc Butte Chateau, an amazing park with waterfalls, caves, and some incredible people watching, I was filled with memories of those times and that amazing, very rainy weekend with Patricia when we saw Paul McCartney.

It was interesting to think how different my life is now, I am now, compared to those bygone times. It was powerful to stand exactly where a previous version of myself stood, like walking in the footsteps of a ghost of myself. It was a powerful reminder of how time changes us, how much one can grow; of how I hoped if I ever returned to Paris, the version of myself standing there today would be just as much a spectre as that 21 year-old standing there wide-eyed with anticipation about a future which terrified him.

After marching all over Buttes Chateau, I decided to go visit the Eiffel Tower. It felt a bit silly to spend my time visiting something I've seen a billion times on film, and multiple times in person, but for some reason it called to me, and so I went.

I was so pleased to see it again. I do find it beautiful, and the site of it, as well as the memories of our crazy gang of vagabonds partying like crazy during the Bastille Day festivities the night we arrived, and the picnic and impromptu dance session we had there the next day, gladdened my heart until tears welled up in my eyes.

In fact, I spent most of the day with tears in my eyes. In part, no doubt, due to sheer exhaustion after a very busy week, and in part because of those beautiful memories of people and times which have touched my life. Still, I find myself filled to bursting often these days, more often than usual.

I believe I am really beginning to see growth and change from all the therapy I've been doing. I really feel that the rubber is beginning to meet the road, and since this feeling began to settle in, so began the tears waiting to pounce at the sight of a tiny puppy, or a kind word from a friend, or the thought of a treasured memory. I don't know what connection there is between these two phenomenon, my improvement and my heightened sensitivity, but it is certainly making for some emotional, 95% of it positive, days.

Today was also a good chance to practice the mantra I have designated for this trip.

THE ROAD IS LIFE.

-william wordsworth.[1]

---

[1] This is a misquote. It was actually Jack Kerouac who said this in his novel *On The Road*. "But no matter, the road is life." I don't know why I thought it was William Wordsworth, but I was very certain that he was the author of this quote. It wasn't until after I returned home, re-read my journal, and then looked it up that I realized I had been wrong the whole time.

My perfectionism keeps me so frequently from just being in the moment; from just enjoying the road. It straps blinders on my eyes, and insists I think only of the destination, and perhaps even more detrimentally, how I'll be able to use it, or make something of it.

My perfectionism wants everything to have an end to justify itself, and rejects the notion that some things, maybe most things, are in fact an end in themselves, or at least should be allowed the opportunity to be.

My perfectionism has threatened this trip since the moment I first heard about El Camino in 2011. It wants me to arrive in Santiago at all costs. It wants me to justify this trip. It wants me to structure my thoughts, set timers on my ideas, guarantee a minimum of the quality and quantity of the self-reflection I commit to. It wants me to forget that this journey is its own end; that this very literal road is, in fact, life.

I had to stop myself from begging my thoughts, or my empty, wandering mind, to justify themselves. I was on the verge several times today of hating myself for embarking upon this journey, which would never produce enough answers or understanding or introspection to justify its drain on my time, body, and wallet.

But I'm better now. The rubber, as I said, is beginning to meet the road. I know how to talk back to my perfectionism now. I know his name, and his fears. And today he was battered time and again, with a simple phrase, each time he reared his ugly head.

THE ROAD IS LIFE.

And that goes especially for this one. I will need to remain vigilant, because he'll be back, but I know that this journey is its own end.

I don't know how, or when, or how much, or even <u>IF</u> this Camino will do me any good. But I want to beat my perfectionism until it doesn't speak up anymore during this trip. This road is its own end.

El Camino es la vida, y vale la pena totalmente de su propia existencia.

All my lovin',

— Blake.

Pride

1. I am proud to have been going non-stop all day on essentially no sleep.
2. I am proud that I made such excellent use of the unintended full day in Paris.
3. I am proud that all my body feels good, only a little tired, after marching all over Paris in my full gear.

Gratitude

1. I am grateful for the beautiful weather, which allowed me to fully appreciate the beauty of Paris.
2. I am grateful Julie suggested I visit "Parc Buttes Chaumont," which was a stunning and exciting park.
3. I am grateful to have the privilege to embark upon this journey, which will be something I'll never quite be able to describe.

Day -1

BAYONNE, FRANCE

Sunday, August 20th, 2017
no time recorded

*T*oday has been the second day of killing Time, and though it has been nice, I must admit it has gone by much slower than I would like, and certainly much slower than it did in Paris. This is probably partly because Bayonne is a tiny medieval city, not a bustling metropolis, because, after yet another sleepless night, this time on a bus, I'm even more exhausted than I was yesterday, and partly because my anxiety and excitement about the journey ahead has left me less patient than I was yesterday.

The overnight bus from Paris to Bayonne, a journey southwest of about 10.5 hours, wold have passed without incident were it not for my complete inability to catch a moment's sleep. Normally I sleep like a log on all forms of public transport, but I was seated in the very front of the bus which meant:

1. I had no seats under which to stretch my legs.
2. Seated directly over the tires, I felt every bump on the road.
3. No seats in front of me, all the lights of the oncoming cars were blinding me every three seconds.

So I have learned an important lesson: never sit at the very front of the bus. When we arrived, I ate an apple and a banana, and was fortunate enough to find a public bathroom where I was able to brush and floss my teeth, put on some deodorant, and brush my hair, which made me feel a lot more human.

After a coffee and croissant in a sunny square, I spent the rest of the day wandering in and out of the winding streets of this quaint, beautiful medieval city.

In the morning there was hardly a soul stirring, today being Sunday, afterall, so my stroll along the shuttered boutique shops selling any number of French specialties to beach going tourists was accompanied only by the faint sound of organ playing and hymn signing emanating from the city's gorgeous cathedral, where Sunday service was being held.

I was far less emotional today, and far less pensive/reflective than I normally am, perhaps because I'm <u>just</u> too damn tired to think.

I had the pleasure of visiting a photo exhibition of a series of photos taken during Alfred Hitchcock's first visit to San Sebastian and Bayonne in the 50's when his film, The Cold Sisters, premiered at the San Sebastian Film Festival. The photos were very cool, and it helped kill a solid hour.

I also saw my first pilgrims today. In fact, I saw several, and while I guessed by their get-up, as practical and fashionless as my own, it was the seashells strapped to their backpacks that gave them away.

The seashell is a symbol of this pilgrimage and its routes, and pilgrims often wear one to signal to others that they are also on the journey.

The seashell made it very easy to approach and speak to people, as it gives us something to connect us, so I'd like to get one myself, to help open myself up even more to the people I meet along the way.

Though I was slightly reinvigorated by the sight of these pilgrims, not least because they were twice my age, which, arrogantly, makes me feel slightly more confident in my capacity as a pilgrim, their appearance also awoke in me the fear of not getting a bed tonight when I finally get to Irún. I am desperate for a decent night's sleep. Still, If I have to sleep in a back alley tonight, I think I'll be fine with that, though a shower would really do me good.

I'm generally feeling more and more positive about this journey, but my latest and perhaps greatest concern is my left knee.

...If I didn't know yet that I'm getting old, I certainly do after writing that sentence...

I injured my left knee on May 1st, May Day, in Berlin, when returning home from the festivities at Görlitzer Park. I was eager to get home, and in the darkness I walked full speed into a trailer hitch directly in the soft flesh beneath the kneecap. I could put no pressure on it for a few weeks, but apart from kneeling, it never gave me any trouble.

The kneeling has slowly but surely gotten better, but in the last few days before the trip, I noticed it began hurting a bit when I go up and down stairs.

This same pain is still present, and over the course of the next 30 days, I'm meant to be going up and down any number of hills, mountains, and cathedral steps, which will only magnify and exacerbate the problem.

Still, I'm reminding myself that worry is often a waste of energy. It represents fear of a thing that hasn't happened yet, and often represents fear of a thing that may never happen at all!

Instead of worrying, I'm trying to remind myself that, in the worst case scenario, I get no bed, and my knee will keep hurting.

So, I'll just rent a hostel and buy some walking sticks when I get to San Sebastian.

In the meantime, I'll cross my fingers and hope for the best.

All my lovin',

- Blake.

Day -1

Pride

1. I'm proud that I, once again, made the most of a day of waiting on such little sleep.
2. I'm proud that I approached 2 strangers to ask them where they got their sea shells. I even made the laugh!
3. I'm proud I've kept my worrying to a minimum, and reminded myself multiple times today that the Road is Life.

Gratitude

1. I'm grateful that I had a chance to enjoy such a beautiful city today, which I would never otherwise have visited.
2. I'm grateful I live in a bustling metropolitan city where I always have something new and interesting to do.
3. I'm grateful I get to go on a train ride today.

Day 1

IRÚN → SAN SEBASTIÁN

22 km / 13.67 mi.

Such joy! Finally and truly on the Camino de Santiago!

Last night, I cannot express the relief I felt when a smiling, cap wearing, mustachioed man greeted me at the door of the albergue from a block away. I must truly look like a pilgrim.

"Hola," he screamed through his snow white mustache.

"Hallo," I responded, my subdued German greeting now my default. I'll have to remember to change that. "Please tell me there's a bed with my name on it."

"Si, claro! There's a bed with your name on it!"

I couldn't believe my luck, and the relief I felt was instant and heavy.

I bought a proper guide book from the albergue and before going to sleep, gave the seemingly insufficient guide I printed to a Frenchman I met, who had apparently left the house with everything...everything except his guidebook.

I slept like a baby, apart from having to wake up a few times to change

positions. Another sign of my age. Apparently lying in one position on a bed is now a thing which certain parts of my body, my hips and ass in particular, take as tantamount to a kick from a mule.

This morning I departed after a very brief breakfast, at 6:30, with Leo, the Frenchman to whom I gave my guide.

I was glad to have him with me because I was worried I'd be unable to find the way out of the city. But, there were little yellow arrows showing us the way.

These ubiquitous little arrows, half a day into my trip, have already become happy little companions. Each one so bright, and individually sloppy, smeared across surfaces as varied as the lengths of their tales, and the angle of their points. They pop out of nowhere, slapped on the back of a sign post, wiped across a railing, spread across a stone, and brightly beckon me forward. They remind me sunnily that the way is long, but I'm going the right direction, and that, even if they were my only companions, I'm not walking this journey alone.

Today I walked the entire journey with Leo, who walked at a good pace, and also reminded me to stop every now and then. I have a tendency to walk as hard and fast as I can until I reach the end point, so it was lovely to walk with someone who suggested, for example, that we stop at a beautiful lookout point to write in our journals for a bit. He's lighthearted, friendly, and funny, and made a great partner. Sometimes we walked in silence, sometimes we joked and laughed. It was very easy, and I was glad for the company after two days without having had a real conversation with another human, and for the chance to speak Spanish.

I also found two walking sticks for which I know my knees are very grateful. I decided to name them, since we'll become very close, and named them Emil and Jennifer, after two of my best friends in Berlin. I know they are rooting for me in Berlin, so it strengthens my heart to have them metaphorically supporting me each and every step of El Camino.

Between the sticks, the amethyst given to me by Alon, a stone meant to protect travelers, and the backpack I borrowed from Emma, I feel so much support from so many people who love me, and it makes me all the merrier literally carrying them with me on the journey.

Something else that I've been carrying with me just about every step of the way is The Bee Gees. I listened to a podcast about the secret powers of music, and in it the hosts interviewed someone who teaches a class in

CPR. According to him, it's necessary to pump the victim's chest 100 beats per minute.

Obviously, not everyone carries a metronome in their pocket, so the CPR technicians had to think of a way to help people estimate 100 BPM. As it turns out, the song, "Stayin' Alive," is 100 BPM, and it's something that everyone knows, so they teach their students to pump the victim's chest while thinking about that super groovy, incredibly famous bass line.

That got me thinking: How can I be sure to set my own rhythm on the Camino, and I got to doing some math.

100 BPM $\times \approx$ 2.5 feet (my stride) = 250 feet per minute

250 FPM $\times$ 60 = 15,000 feet per hour

15,000 $\div$ 5,280 = 2.84 miles per hour

Verdict! TOO SLOW.

So, now when I walk, that song is pumping in my head, and I think of how groovy and confident they were in the video and it speeds me right along to a faster stride of approximately four miles per hour.

It also makes me feel closer to my mom, who would be thrilled to know that The Bee Gees are with me literally every step of the way.

Today's only day one, and while I have a long way to go, today helped me to see that this journey is well within my reach. Today I finally felt the confidence that, yes, this will be hard, but I can do it!

Day 1

And barring unforeseen circumstances, I shall.

Only about 800 more kilometers to go.

All my lovin',

- Blake.

Pride

1. I'm proud I completed the first day of El Camino.
2. I'm proud that I'm being really social, and am unafraid to speak with anyone I meet!
3. I'm proud that my body is in quite good shape, and is getting me where it should
4. I'm proud that I was brave enough to do Tai Chi on a beach full of people with a group of youngsters laughing at me the whole time.

Gratitude

1. I'm grateful that I had Leo to walk with today.
2. I'm grateful that my body is strong and healthy enough to carry me down El Camino
3. I'm grateful that the beach in San Sebastian was fresh, and that I could return to the Ocean!
4. I'm grateful that the older gentleman in the city helped me find a kebab shop.

Day 2

SAN SEBASTIÁN → ZARAUTZ

19 km / 11.8 mi.

Today I woke at 5:00, and was out on El Camino by 5:30. It was a wonderful day.

Climbing high into the hills on the West side of San Sebastián, I watched the Sun rise up behind the hills on the East side of the city. It almost looked like the hills were on fire, the massive statue of Jesus atop the peak, only a silhouette against the morning light, looking down, hands open, watching idly as the blaze approached.

I spent today walking alone, and apart from a few minutes and the time to have coffee and tortilla in Ondía with two guys I met at the albergue yesterday, my walk was a solitary one. And I thoroughly enjoyed it. I even found myself half dancing and singing, "Stayin' Alive," in my highest falsetto.

My therapist and I discussed this before I left. The hope that some solitude on El Camino would help me learn to truly enjoy being alone; to truly enjoy my own company, and understand that time with myself is as wonderful and enjoyable as time spent with others.

Of course, now that I think about it, it's no surprise that I've always

hated being alone, and avoided it at all costs. The number of times I spent hopping from coffee with this friend, a beer with that friend, a film with that friend, a meal with that acquaintance, a skype call with a family member back home, pushing that inevitable moment where I had only my thoughts to accompany me…

…Like a child trying his hardest to delay his obligatory return home at day's end where he knows his alcoholic father sits chain smoking at the kitchen table, waiting to take his day out on someone smaller and weaker than himself.

Who could ever love spending time alone with a self that knows only how to lash out angrily, irrationally, violently, relentlessly at the only victim who can't say "no?", who can't fight back?

I finally am beginning to understand why alone time has always been so dreaded...I've always been the kind of company you come to expect from an abusive husband. I've spent a lifetime being so cruel to myself. This realization has literally brought tears to my eyes.

It hurts to know how poorly I've treated myself. Deeply...the way it hurts to know how much time one has wasted on an undeserving partner whose neglect and cruelty finally drove one out the front door, duffel bag in hand, stuffed with whatever physical manifestations of a life were within reach.

But today marks an incredible turning point in that life I've lived, in that relationship with myself. My therapy helped me see who I was living with, showed me it was time to pack my bags and leave that undeserving version of myself behind.

As I discussed with Michael, my therapist, this trip was that opportunity, now freed from a relationship with myself that wasn't serving me well, to find a partnership with that side of myself that I give to everyone else; that smart, fun, happy, loving, caring, giving part of myself. And I believe today marked the start of that partnership.

I don't remember even what I was thinking but at some point early in the morning I burst into laughter; roaring belly laughter, and said out loud, "Oh, Jesus <u>CHRIST</u> I am <u>funny</u>!"

I spent the rest of the Camino laughing, singing, dancing down the road, truly enjoying being with myself in a way I don't think I ever have.

Zarautz is a small beach town with the largest beach in this region. Like yesterday in San Sebastián, the albergue is a stone's throw away from the beach, and like yesterday, as soon as we were given beds, I threw

down my things, put on my swimsuit, and headed straight to the sea.

The water is clear, and reflects a glassy, frosty aquamarine. The waves today were <u>incredible</u>. INCREDIBLE!

I haven't seen waves like this sense I went to the Mud Festival in South Korea in 2010.

They were massive, but not dangerous; manageable, but threatening, the biggest danger being hurtled into a small child basking in the surf.

I could hardly contain myself. Body surfing is one of my most loved activities in the entire world. There's nothing like it. I never stop. I'm like a dog playing fetch, still bounding while his master has long since tired of throwing. I dive with the waves time and again, and before I've even been deposited in the sand, hair draped over my face like a swamp creature emerging from the deep, I'm leaping back into the breakers, digging into the water to propel myself against the tide, making every effort to snag each and every worthwhile wave. It is, for me, pure, unadulterated joy. I must seem like a man possessed to the people around me. I shout, I scream, I curse when I miss, and I laugh maniacally when I feel the wave lift me into its peak, and shriek with joy when I'm flung on the beach like so much jetsam and flotsam.

I've been watching the waves roll in for the last hour as I write this, endless streams of Spaniards strolling along the stone promenade, partners, families, friends, seemingly unaware of the late hour on what is ostensibly a school night. It's been a joy to be part of, a banging soundtrack including Brown Eyed Girl, Like a Rolling Stone, Mrs. Robinson, Anything You Want, Fire and Rain, and every other beachy hit in the genre, locals singing in thick accents as they pass by, words a slur of poorly comprehended English, playing from the terrace bar where everyone is drinking.

It has truly been difficult to keep myself from jumping into the sea and continue catching waves. If I were more certain Spaniards were as okay with nudity as Germans, I'd go in naked.

But I keep reminding myself, I must try to rest and save some energy. I have a long road ahead, and a left knee which is almost certain to give me gradually more trouble as the journey continues, and potentially for a long time after...I realized today that I have passed that age where aches and pains coming and going is a given. I've entered the realm of crossing certain beloved activities off my list of hobbies due to physical maladies which I bestowed recklessly upon myself back in that era when I could still take my health for granted.

I have to return to the albergue before the doors shut at 22:00. I hope the waves have worn me out enough to sleep. I'm sleeping very poorly, waking every hour.

If not, no bother. Tomorrow starts at 5:00, and the Camino to Deba awaits.

All my lovin',

— Blake.

Day 2

Pride

1. I am proud that I got up at 5:00 AM and headed straight out of the albergue
2. I am proud that I completed the 1st step by myself, and was smiling the whole way
3. I am proud that I practiced the three P's to keep from ruminating about commenting on the age of 71 year old Jacob, whom I met on El Camino. I was embarrassed about what I'd said to him and had to stop my head from looping.

Gratitude

1. I am grateful for the delicious tortilla and café I had in Ondía today.
2. I am grateful for the amazing waves in Zarautz today! BODY SURF!!!
3. I am grateful for the lovely people I'm meeting already on El Camino

Day 3

ZARAUTZ → DEBA

23 km / 14.29 mi.

Wednesday, August 23rd, 2017

22:15

The life of the pilgrim is very simple.

Wake.
Walk.
Wash self.
Wash clothes.
Wait.
Sleep.
Repeat.

I suppose it's this simplicity that makes it so beautiful; that makes the pilgrim open himself/herself to new thoughts and new people. There's really nothing else to distract you from the people you meet along the way, and the things that pop into your head.

This simplicity truly lightens the spiritual load on the heart. Travel, for all the ways in which it is glorified, is actually quite stressful. There's always a bus to catch, or a flight to get to, or an item that might be

robbed, or luggage to be lost.

But on the Camino, these burdens don't exist. I have nothing worth stealing, unless there's a rogue thief with a dirty sock fetish roaming the Camino. There's no transport to worry about missing, unless your feet might wander off without you. There's no need to worry about getting lost, unless you never learned how arrows work, and what they mean. There's nothing to do but walk, and nowhere to be except on El Camino.

Such simplicity is a rarity and such prolonged simplicity is unheard of.

Day 3

The only real concern is how to fill the time between arriving at the albergue, and crawling gleefully into your sleeping bag, and frankly, I have found that time incredibly easy to fill.

Firstly, everything takes much longer than usual. Body and mind arrive to the albergue so worn down that neither is functioning at more than 60% capacity. Everything is done slowly, carefully, in a sleepy daze. It's only after I find myself stopping for the third time in the middle of a task to ask myself, "Wait...what was I doing?" that I think I realize how tired I am. It's only when I realize that what I was doing was looking worriedly for one of my items, each a precious tool vital for my journey, which I had in my hand the whole time, that I actually realize how tired I am.

The sloth-like movements of life between arrival and sleep still find a rhythm, a ritual, a routine. Humans love routines.

So after arriving, washing, I have still so much I want to do before bed.

Meditate for 10 minutes
Tai Chi for 30 minutes
Walk around and explore the city for a bit
Write in my Camino Journal.
Pride & Gratitude journal.
Swim in the ocean
Talk to People
Edit and organize my photos.
Slowly enjoy a well deserved beer.

It's a struggle to get it all in, but what a beautiful struggle it is:

Literally fill your day with things you love.
Every day for 35 days.

What a pleasure, what a series of simple, sweet pleasures this journey is.

Today was a hard walk. The road was the easiest yet, but I was feeling weak and tired after 5 days of fairly intense travel, and as many utterly sleepless nights.

Still, it was a wonderful day. I feel so open and free to be myself. I stop and meet everyone I pass. I know the name of so many people I pass, or meet in the hostel. I am beginning to lose that anxiety that has gripped every social interaction for so long.

The need to dampen my personality for the benefit of the people I encounter feels left behind in Irún, along with my desperate desire to please and make people love me.

I am beginning to wear my skin comfortably, confidently, compassionately.

This is who I am. I hope you like it.

If not, I won't apologize, but I understand, and I invite you to seek a more fitting interaction.

This is who I am, and it is who I am going to be. Because it is who I desire to be.

And in spite of this unapologetic approach to being myself, I've never felt more warmly received, or more genuinely appreciated.

"So, how many names did you get today?" I was asked.

"Do you know everyone on this Camino?" I was asked.

I'm beginning to feel like I do. And I'm beginning to allow them to know me, just as I'm beginning to really know myself.

I bought a knee brace today, and cured my first blister. The Camino is difficult, and everything hurts, from my feet to my hands to my shoulders. And it is really a joy.

I have to remind myself to write about a lesson in compassion I was given today.

I swam in the gorgeous water on Deba's tiny beach for a solid hour, and drank three beers with Olivia, a Ukranian woman my age with whom I will attempt to walk 31 KM (19.26 mi.) tomorrow for the chance to sleep in a monastery, in the hopes of wearing myself out so I can sleep.

I'm the last of the 50 people in this albergue still awake.

I pray I can finally sleep tonight.

If not, El Camino will be waiting for me at 5:00 AM anyway.

I can't wait.

All my lovin',

- Blake.

Day 3

Pride

1. I'm proud that I successfully treated a blister mid-Camino today.
2. I'm proud that I enjoyed time alone with myself.
3. I'm proud that so many countless people have stopped mid-sentence to remark upon how well I speak Spanish.

Gratitude

1. I'm grateful for the guidebook which taught me to treat blisters.
2. I'm grateful that the ocean was so beautiful and warm today.
3. I'm grateful for Spanish coffee. Christ, it is delicious.

Day 4

DEBA → MONASTARIO DE ZENNARUZA

31 km / 19.26 mi.

I'm tired to the core of my bones. Another sleepless night, capped off with the worst nightmare I've had in a long time. It involved a lot of bizarre moments of my friends on drugs and dancing to strange music, none of whom looked like they should. I fought fiercely with a friend with whom I left a bit of a loose end untied before I left. Fury and ferocity, and rage over a musician with whom I'm completely enchanted. She was kissing my cheek and whispering in my ear as my friend screamed wildly at me with fire in his eyes when my alarm went off at 5:00. I was happy to have to get up.

Olivia and I were out the door by 5:30, hoping to arrive at a monastery 31 KM (19.26 mi.) away where there were only 21 beds. We walked into the forest in darkness, making our way slowly along with the aid of her head lamp, basking in the silence and silhouettes.

Today was the most beautiful, wildest, and most difficult of them all. The knee brace and Olivia's pace, slower than my natural run, helped keep the pain down, and the way enjoyable.

We pass Camino amigo after Camino amigo. At this point I feel we know everyone on the road, and I'm gladdened each time I encounter them, or they encounter me.

The hills today were steep and massive, demanding patience due to the steep angle of the incline and the rockyness of the path circumscribing them.

There was a fantastical ambience as a thick mist sat thickly and heavily in the mountains. Our journey created its own organic soundtrack, the rhythmic stomping of our boots and tapping of our sticks accompanied by the lowing of cattle, the bleating of sheep, and accented by the occasional hollow ringing of a tiny cowbell strapped around the neck of some farm animal hobbling nimbly down the hills somewhere in the fog.

Tonight we will sleep in an old monastery where we'll be given a hot meal, the first I'll have had since I left Berlin. The journey here was very difficult, but it's wonderful to be a part of. I'm certain there will be a day, and soon, where I won't feel this joy, but for the moment the pain is part of the pleasure.

How quickly having little has boosted my appreciation of the small things. Today while brushing my teeth, a showering pilgrim had music playing. The song was one I like very much, and the opening notes nearly made me cry. So did a cup of coffee I drank yesterday.

I finally had a chance to walk a bit of El Camino with Jacob, a 71 year-old Canadian from Ontario with whom I have crossed paths every day. He has won the award for most interesting pilgrim I've met thus far. His accent and manner of speaking are exactly like my dad's, which makes me feel closer to home.

This is his second Camino, having walked the Camino Frances last year. In the last five KM, which were very difficult, the power and rhythm of his walking sticks striking the road kept us all moving forward, like the beat of a galley drum. We all said so.

He sold a business of making molds for plastics 12 years after starting it at 34, and from 46 he's been retired and living off that same business. He's a world record holder in rowing marathons for people over 55. He has story after story which he is happy to tell, and I'm happy to listen to. His icy green eyes belie a friendly, humble intellect, and a wisdom gained from living the dream.

Today I had to learn to listen to my body. My knee won't let me go as fast as I want, and it frustrates me. I want to be the master that my body must follow, but today my body was the master that I had to follow. And while I started the day cursing my leg and my bad luck, I quickly remembered that I'm here to learn.

There's no sense in that anger I felt. "If my fucking knee were okay, I'd be flying down the camino."

Yes, you would. But it isn't. So now what?

Go slower. Respect your pain. Take this excuse to go slower, and appreciate the incredible scene unfolding around you.

So I did. And I was happier for it.

I meditated in the silence of this small, beautiful church, and did Tai Chi in the Cloiture. I drank a beer made here at the monastery in the garden.

I lost my Pilgrim Passport; left it in the hostel in Deba. I'll try to have them mail it to me. Otherwise I lose my lovely hostel stamps forever.

I forgave myself quickly. I <u>hate</u> losing things. How irresponsible. But I remembered that I'm not here to collect stamps. I'm here to learn in part to love myself. And that means forgiving myself when I've made a mistake, or had an accident. Which I did.

Poco a Poco. Baby Steps.

All my lovin',

- Blake.

Day 4

Pride

1. I'm proud of the fact that I walked 31 KM (19.26 mi.) today.
2. I'm proud of some of the wonderful photos I've taken.
3. I'm proud of my steps down the road to loving myself the way I love others.

Gratitude

1. I'm grateful for the magnificent views I had today.
2. I'm grateful for the excellent company I'm finding on the road.
3. I'm grateful for the pasta I'll eat tonight.

Day 5

MONASTARIO DE ZENNARUZA → ESKERIKA

26 km / 16.16 mi.

*A*nother wonderful day on the camino, after another sleepless night. At the monastery we were given coffee and bread for breakfast, which we ate on the terrace while a pink sky slowly illuminated above the jagged black line of the mountains.

I began the day walking with Jacob. For two hours we traded stories and laughs. He is the epitome of the person I was hoping to meet. Someone who has had a wildly successful life in a completely unorthodox way. I take great inspiration in him and the life he has lived, and am terribly glad for his company, at once so warm, light, and familiar.

Having walked the extra KM to the monastery, we were many KM ahead of the majority of our wave of pilgrims in Marinka, so this morning the trails through sweet pueblos and beautiful mountain forests were ours alone.

I decided to leave Jacob a little and walk on my own for a while in the silence of the Camino. It was magical.

Interestingly, I thought the solitude of the Camino is where my thoughts would have their origins, but in fact it isn't the case. The road is difficult and rocky, and a sprained ankle or twisted knee is waiting around every crooked step. El Camino demands respect and all your attention if one hopes to arrive safely.

Still, today, as I walked alone, having warded off a brief bout with irrational anxiety, something occurred to me. Had I done El Camino either of the times in the past when I considered it, it would have ended horribly. It wasn't the right time in my life which makes me glad I didn't do it then, due to those unforeseen circumstances which got in the way.

I can imagine the rancor and bitterness and fear I would have carried with me on the road at those times in my life. I can see with incredible clarity the ease with which those nagging lifelong concerns, those familiar, unprocessed traumas, that black shroud of uncertainty and self loathing would have enveloped the entire journey; would have crept in to fill every nook and cranny of the moments walking alone on the road. It would have had the opposite effect of this journey, in which thanks to therapy and life experience, I find myself secure and full of comprehension about my bad mental habits, and armed with the tools I need to combat them. And that clarity leaves me free to enjoy the solitude of the road, the time alone with myself, and all the feelings and emotions that come crawling out of the woodworks when I arrive at the albergue, too tired to uphold the emotional defense mechanisms which keep so many thoughts at bay in the normal day to day.

I would have stopped today after 16 KM (9.94 mi.) in Gernika, but hearing that familiar CLICK CLACK of Jacob's sticks pass by the albergue, I knew he would continue the 10 KM to the next albergue. I got up, put on my shoes, grabbed my bag, and carried on, called by the energy of his steps.

Day 5

The albergue is wonderful. I did Tai chi with Sean, and we all 12 ate a meal cooked by Leo, who was just as picky and cantankerous a cook as a Frenchman is meant to be. It was amazing.

26 KM (16.16 mi.) till Bilbao, where there are massive fiestas.

All my lovin',

- Blake.

Pride

1. I'm proud of all the compliments Emil gave me for Bottle Up and Explode. "Guitar playing was excellent!"
2. I'm proud I walked 10 KM (6.21 mi.) more than anticipated because I followed my gut and did what I wanted.
3. I'm proud that I helped organize a massive dinner for everyone at the albergue.

Gratitude

1. I'm grateful that Mario shared his joint with me last night.
2. I'm grateful that I enjoyed my alone time on the road so much.
3. I'm grateful that the Deba tourist office found my Pilgrim Passport and is mailing it to Germany.

Day 6

ESKERIKA → BILBAO

23 km / 14.29 mi.

Saturday, August 26th, 2017

16:34

Today was a fairly easy day, and, while it was lovely and silent in the forest as we left the Albergue, we quickly entered an industrial district leading into the large city of Bilbao. While my knees were thrilled for the certainty of the asphalt and the relatively flat lay of the land, it was certainly the ugliest day of the camino.

We picked up a new member of our little camino family. Abigail, a tall, thin woman with bright blue eyes and a delightful Danish accent as light and innocent as her playful spirit. She's a joy to walk with. She keeps a steady pace, and has the gift of the gab. We walked together this morning and Olivia and Jacob caught up with us when we stopped for a coffee and a snack.

I have little to say and few thoughts I feel inclined to write about. It's still lovely, and there is a real warmth to the group identity of the pilgrims.

The albergues close their doors and turn out their lights at 22:00, so we all go to bed together, we all rise together, and you'll always wind up walking with a few of them. Then we arrive at the albergue one by one, and wait for the doors to open at 15:00.

This is my favorite part of the day. Everyone's energy is renewed after showers and washing. It's so exciting to see who will show up, and the energy is always bright and positive at this time, as everyone tends to their feet and discusses their experience along the Camino.

Going to sleep is also really comforting. Everyone is together, and it feels like a big sleepover. Everyone wishes each other good night and slowly but surely deep breaths of peaceful, desperately needed sleep erupt from the bunks in all directions. Even the inevitable freight-train-snoring from one pilgrim or the other doesn't disrupt the peacefulness of resting with all these people, dirty, and tired, and weary, and deeply satisfied with the journey, just like me. Just like all the other pilgrims.

Tonight is special because there are massive parties all week in Bilbao to celebrate the city's origins. The Albergue will be open until midnight so we can see the fireworks and enjoy the parties!

Tomorrow is another light day, and our Camino will carry us back to the sea, which I have missed these last three days.

I got a new credential at the cathedral, and feel like an official pilgrim again.

All my lovin',

- Blake.

Day 1

BILBAO → POBAÑO

24 km / 16.16 mi.

Sunday, August 27th, 2017.
17:35 PM

*B*ilbao was an absolute treat! I went to Bilbao years ago with Stefano, Jonas, and Juan on our Hippy Road Trip in 2009, just long enough to visit the Guggenheim Museum before we continued driving onward to San Sebastián. But yesterday we had plenty of time to enjoy the city. And there was a lot to enjoy!

Jacob, Olivia, Abigail, and I, after taking a couple of hours to clean, write, and plan the next stages of our journey, spent the afternoon walking to the Guggenheim before heading back to the city center, right by our albergue, for dinner and festivities.

Even though we ate a delicious late lunch while waiting for the albergue to open, we were all starving again by 18:00. According to Leo's watch, we're burning over 2,300 calories a day on the day's journeys alone. It's difficult to eat enough during the day, and in spite of the fact that I'm snacking all day on nuts, fruits, chocolates, and the occasional tapa, I'm always hungry, and definitely losing weight.

My bathing suit was practically falling off today, and my usual, hard-earned 4-pack has turned into a 6-pack for the first time since I was 21! I never thought I'd see the day! I'd better get some pictures to preserve the memories of my fortunately very healthy youth.

So, El Camino makes eating lots a must, and allows us all to glutton without a single trace of guilt.

We had such trouble finding a place to eat. We were in a big Plaza where there was a traditional Basque band playing flutes and banging snare drums while a leader called out dance moves in <u>Euskera</u> (the local language of the Basque) and dozens of people danced traditional folk dances involving spinning, clapping, snapping, fancy footwork in unison in a big circle, all while observing an apparent "no smiling" rule. The cheesiness of it all was excellent.

The Plaza was surrounded by tapas bars, but all the tables and chairs were occupied, so we drank beers and hunted for a free table, which required patience because Spaniards can occupy a table with a single beer for hours.

We eventually got a table smashed between hordes of people, and got ourselves 12 pintxos (Basque Tapas) to share. They were tasty, but not enough to fill us up, so we decided to have a Pintxos Party, and gathered our stuff and went to a bar next door where we got another 12 pintxos and had a magnificent feast, enveloped on all sides by laughter, bar hubbub, the whistling of the folk music from the plaza on the left, and the banging of street drummers from the alley on the right.

It was impossible to speak, but it was just as well, as it forced us to really focus on the enjoyment of our food. These pintxos were magnificent, elaborate, artisanal works of art stacked atop tiny slices of toasted baguette. We were mostly uncertain of what we were eating, but the combinations of sauces, meats, fish, eggs, and vegetables were as beautiful as they were bursting with intriguing flavors.

When we finished all the miniature masterpieces, our curiosity was still unsatisfied, and our hunger threatened to linger. What else were we to do but get more Pintxos?!

All totalled, dinner was seven pintxos and two beers each, for a total of about €15.00. Not bad at all.

While it was initially a bit stressful because we were all so hungry and I was afraid people's patience was wearing thin, the dinner is one of my favorite, most fun memories from El Camino so far.

Bellies full and hearts gladdened, we took our beers to the dancing people and laughed and laughed.

Jacob went back home, but not before his capacity for beer consumption could impress me as much as his ability to out-walk me on the Camino, and Abigail, Olivia, and I spent the rest of the night drinking and wandering the streets full of people enjoying live music, break dancing, street performers, and, of course, folk dancing. We eventually were brave enough to jump in briefly, which was hilarious.

The night ended with a delightful fireworks show, after which we wandered back to the albergue where I slept the sweet sleep of the drunken and weary, the first night's sleep I've had since I left Berlin nearly ten days ago.

When we left the albergue at 7:00, what would have been a peaceful stroll through a quiet, empty Bilbao, it's residents enjoying a long, slow Sunday sleep, was replaced with an absolute shit show; a mess of people wandering aimlessly through the streets screaming, hollering, laughing with a volume only Spaniards are capable of. The streets were littered with piles of bottles, wrappers, empty plastic cups, pizza boxes, the butts of sandwiches whose insides had been consumed, the ends left to the birds, and any other manner of party detritus, evidence of the ferocity of the festivities, all being swept into piles by city employees spraying the sidewalks, still full of people showing no signs of stopping, with fire hoses, where they would later be gobbled up by tractors made for eating garbage.

We were all dying laughing as we tried to escape the veritable Bedlam by which we were surrounded. Spaniards party long, but not hard. Most won't be drunk at any point in the night, though they'll have a drink in their hand the entire night. They'll slowly drink sip by sip, just enough to stay merry and energized, but nothing more.

The people we passed, people of all ages young and old, all looked remarkably fresh considering they'd been out all night, apart from the occasional girl crying in a corner of the fiesta, consoled by a slightly miffed boyfriend, victim of emotions overstimulated by a few drinks too many. It was just as I remembered the Magdalena fiestas in Castellón, except I was in a state of mind to truly appreciate the mess I was observing this time.

Today, our walk was through a barren industrial wasteland along the river for the first 13 KM (8.08 mi.). I was happy for the flat terrain, a break my knee badly needed, but my hips suffered from the constant shock from the pavement and asphalt. It made me grateful for the verdant cities I have always had the pleasure of calling home.

We missed Olivia today, who decided to stay in Bilbao to visit the Guggenheim. I hope she'll catch up to us and continue the road to Santiago at our pace soon.

I've met two people on this trip who have lost someone extremely close to them to suicide. It's strange. I've considered suicide many times in my life, with varying degrees of seriousness, as early as 12 years old, and as recently as a few short weeks ago. I have a great deal of empathy for those who have succumb to suicide. Yet, I was shocked and deeply saddened to hear these stories of tragic loss.

I was surprised by how much it hurt to hear about these suicides, and I think it's because I've come so far in my therapy and personal development of late.

I feel I have genuinely turned a corner, and feel as though, come what may, on my new path, the potential for the viability of, the potential for resorting to suicide, has vanished around the bend I have left behind, as I head for greener pastures beyond my new horizon.

Having finally come to a place where suicide will never again be even a remote option, the knowledge of these suicides has hit hard because I know it was likely they could have been prevented. I thought I'd never see the day when I didn't have suicide packed away as a Plan B. Now that I have reached that place, I know it is possible for many, even those who suffer from deep, severe, frequent depression.

The confusion about the pain I felt as a result of these tales of suicide got me thinking about why I felt them so deeply, and brought about this realization that I have left that mental state behind.

I have come so far, and for that I am truly grateful.

All my lovin',

-Blake.

Day 7

Pride

1. I am proud that I swam in the ocean after a tiring day of walking.
2. I am proud that I made the Catalan family laugh so hard all day in Spanish! I'm funny in foreign languages!
3. I'm proud that the hospitalero thought I was a native Spanish speaker from Spain!

Gratitude

1. I am grateful that my Camino family has been so loving, fun, and easy.
2. I am grateful that the rain fell today <u>AFTER</u> we finished our journey.
3. I'm grateful that I got to swim on such a beautiful beach today.

Day 8

POBAÑO → LIENDO

37 km / 22.99 mi.

The scenery has been less than idyllic since we neared Bilbao and entered Cantabria. This morning involved a lot of walking along the highway and although we've returned to the sea, between the cars screaming along beside us, and the industry inhabiting property no one would ever want for their home, it hasn't exactly been what I was looking for in my solitary walks through the Spanish countryside.

We walked 37 KM (22.99 mi.) today and although it was long and hard, the amazing breakfast we had and the gorgeous, green mountainous Cantabrian countryside we walked through on the last 12 or so KM (7.46 mi.) made it a wonderful journey.

No major revelations today, except that I am going to insist that my parents get their passports and come visit me in Europe. I'm tired of them having no understanding of the life I live, and I can feel the resentment is growing. So, I'll do something about it now.

Tonight was hilarious. Jacob, Abigail, Leo and I drank beer at a local bar in this VERY tiny village, the only bar, I think, in a delirious fit of laughter, and then Leo cooked us a pasta carbonara while teaching me to say, "The water is boiling," in Italian, which I repeated hundreds of times, pointing at things that were very clearly not boiling.

My Camino Love finally arrived. Samantha, a gorgeous Italian woman from Rome, a sweet, funny, charming Nurse, literally took my breath away when I saw her. She's going to walk with us tomorrow morning. How exciting!

All my lovin',

- Blake.

Day 8

Pride

1. I'm proud that I walked over 37 KM (22.99 mi.) today, almost non-stop
2. I'm proud that so many people complimented my Spanish, and were even confused about where I came from.
3. I'm proud that I kept Jacob, Leo, and Abigail cracking up so hard all day today after we arrived to the albergue.

Gratitude

1. I'm grateful that we somehow avoided the rain all day today.
2. I'm grateful that the people I'm walking with are so kind and generous and funny.
3. I'm grateful that I'm learning to truly enjoy my own company.
4. I'm grateful that Leo cooked us dinner again.

Day 9

LIENDO → GÜEMES

35 km / 21.75 mi.

*A*nother very long day today! 35 KM (21.75 mi.)! Luckily, the terrain was fairly easy, apart from the mountain path which was very narrow, rocky, and slippery from the rain and all the asphalt we walked on, which, though steady and easy, is killer on the soles of the feet and hips.

Thankfully, the distance was made easier by the beauty of the journey. Today was incredibly varied, and began with a quiet stroll through insignificant, quaint mountain pueblos connected by verdant hills, and surrounded by mountains shrouded in morning mist as thick and thorough as the web a spider uses to encase its prey.

After descending into Laredo, not before stopping to admire the breathtaking view, we walked along 5 KM (3.11 mi.) of uninterrupted beach bordered by glassy sea, before taking a fairy across a small channel to the tiny city of Satoña. There we stopped for breakfast before continuing on to kilometers more of beach and a treacherous mountain pass, whose difficult crossing was rewarded with spectacular ocean views in all directions.

The next 15 KM (9.32 mi.) were spent passing through rolling green hills peppered with terracotta rooftops, patches of evergreen forest,

cornfields, and bejeweled with an imposing cathedral every few kilometers. Cantabria is gorgeous.

As well, the Sun was shining and the sky was blue, which has been a rarer sight than I would have imagined in Spain, but I suppose a place this green is no stranger to clouds and rainfall.

The way was long, and when we arrived at the famous hostel, notorious for its eccentric Hospitalero and the communal meals capped off with singing and music, I was wrecked.

After a shower, which was one of the best I've had on the Camino, I found myself exhausted, impatient, and grumpy. It was the worst I've felt since I started the walk.

I was a bit overwhelmed by the 60+ pilgrims walking around the gorgeous white farmhouse boasting beautiful gardens and lovely countryside views, and in no mood to fraternize.

It was a really unpleasant sense of deep crankiness which certainly threatened to turn South quickly, so I was glad to see my therapy snapping into action.

"Okay, what are you feeling?" I asked myself.

"Tired, grumpy and antisocial...and grumpy," I responded.

Having named the emotions and feelings made it easier to think of some solutions.

"Grab your journal, some chocolate, and your bottle of water. Find a quiet place. We'll meditate, write our Pride and Gratitude, then eat some lovely chocolate for a boost of sugar, and a little medicine for the heart. Then move to the garden for Tai Chi. After that, we'll write in the journal."

It was good to have a plan, but as I began my Tai chi, I found my mood mostly unchanged, weak form the intense physical activity of the day, my mind was very susceptible to the tricks of the darkness which is still knocking about in there, whose grip was proving difficult to slip. I allowed it to tighten its hold, and whisper to me.

"All that therapy, and here we are. Still feeling bad, still feeling weak and an outcast. Maybe it's all for naught. Maybe you're a lost cause. This Camino was a terrible idea. Day 9 and you're ready to quit. You're in one of the nicest albergues on the Camino, and you're feeling like shit. This may well be the rest of your night..the rest of your life."

I was distracted from these intermittent jabs at my newfound optimism as I moved through the form, but they crept in again and again.

"STOP." I told myself. "None of that is true." The words of Dr. Tal Ben-Shahar, psychologist and personal savior, rang out in the darkness of that space between my ears.

"Permission to be human. You're tired and grumpy, just as most people would be after 35 KM (21.75 mi.) in the Sun. You won't be forever, but you're allowed to be now. You're working to calm yourself. Continue the form. Focus on the movement of the form. Breathe. Relax."

I continued the form with renewed concentration, then ran through it again, stretching my muscles, and trying to avoid that pain in my knee.

By the time I was done, I felt better. I grabbed some peanuts, as dinner was a while away, and drank lots of water, and began writing from a terrace with a magnificent view, and a spotted dog nibbling at my ankles and everything else within his reach.

Between the calories, the countryside, and the physical manifestation of my emotions via ink on paper, the darkness has been overpowered and returned to the depths of my mind where it awaits, plotting it's next attack. I'm proud I came out on top today.

It's very important for me to remember: I'm not in therapy to eradicate the possibility of negative thoughts, feelings, and emotions. That's impossible. I'm in therapy to become stronger than the darkness. The darkness will always be there, but as I get stronger it'll get weaker, and I'll triumph over it faster and with greater ease every time.

That's what I'm doing, and I'm doing it well, and I'm proud of my progress.

Day 9

And that's what this camino has provided me: the time to reflect on, practice, and cement these tools I'm building for myself without the distraction of the rest of my daily life impeding the progress.

I feel much better, and am very excited about the evening ahead of me.

All my lovin',

– Blake.

Pride

1. I'm proud that my body is holding up so well on this trip. I'm in good shape!
2. I'm proud that I'm staying present and catching my bad thoughts and feelings, and reacting in a way to get me out of those feelings.
3. I'm proud I'm making friends with such nice people.

Gratitude

1. I'm grateful for the chocolate, which I'm eating to cure my grumpiness.
2. I'm grateful that we will be served dinner tonight, and that it smells so good!
3. I'm grateful that I have a quiet place to meditate for a little while.

Day 10

GÜEMES → BOO DE PIÉLAGOS

30 km / 18.64 mi.

Day 10

Wednesday, August 30th, 2017

19:09

Today was my first angry moment on El Camino. After breakfast at the albergue in Güemes, where the coffee was wonderful and abundant, we had an astounding walk along Cantabrian cliffs dropping dramatically into the roaring crystal clear sea walloping the rocks a hundred feet below.

Upon arriving on the outskirts of Somo, a quiet little port town, we descended onto the beach where we would need to walk for several kilometers along the sea, directly in the sand in order to get to the town itself, from which we would take a ferry to Santander.

Walking across the sand in trekking gear and with kilos of bags on our backs proved quite difficult, so we walked down by the water where the sand was harder from the surf. Between constantly kicking sand in my shoes/socks, and worrying about the damage that sand would do to my feet throughout the day, and the sheer difficulty of walking through the sand bow legged to avoid kicking more sand into my shoes, not to mention the hunger in my belly, and the seemingly unending beach trek that still lay ahead of us, I was getting pretty fed up and frustrated. To further complicate the matter, the waves were constantly leaping at my feet, forcing me to walk like a drunken seagull along the surf, with none

of the agility of a seagull as it shoots in and out of the surf.

Of course, eventually, the surf washed over my right shoe, soaking it. No matter. One wet foot on an easy day would be fine. I continued my graceless game of cat and mouse with the surf, forcing more sand into my heels until finally a rogue wave completely covered both feet, and soaked immediately to my skin. The only word that my brain could remember of all 5 languages I speak, the only world left in the thesaurus of my brain was, "FUCK." And as it was the only word I had to express myself, I felt it necessary to repeat it over and over. Loudly, forcefully, and with rage and anger and all my distaste for the gracelessness of this stretch of the walk.

Abigail witnessed it all, but said nothing. After a moment, she came beside me and said tenderly through a smirk, "that's it. That's the first bad moment of the Camino."

"That's it," I said. What made me angriest was how obvious it was that I should have just removed my shoes, walked in the sea, and washed them when I got off the beach in the beach showers.

Not only would that have been more efficient, that would have been hilarious and really fun. I would have LOVED that 3 KM (1.86 mi.) stretch of the camino.

"Okay," she said, "we're almost dere," and we stomped up the beach to the showers.

I was so pleased to see that I was able to let it go. Just accept that I did nothing wrong, that now I learned the best way to cross the beach, no matter how short it seems, or how fast you want to go, take the time to take off the shoes and enjoy the water, which is better anyway!

While the lesson itself is pretty insignificant in the grand scheme of my life, the process behind it carries more weight. The ability to express anger, accept it, move on, and be laughing and singing again is massive.

That same thing a year ago would have ruined hours of my day, if not the entire thing, and soured my dreams, and the knock on effects of that type of profound negativity, both chemical and spiritual, would have lingered into the next day to continue perpetuating the force behind my slide into the darkness.

But not today. And while at the time I was pleased to see that I had recovered so quickly, the immensity of what I had just done didn't occur to me until I wrote it down.

Immediately thereafter came another victory.

While washing my feet in the shower and changing socks, I was singing, "Be With You," by Mr. Big, a song played in the albergue by the Hospitalero in Bilbao as we got ready to leave in the morning, which has become a kind of anthem for this trip.

I was singing and joking and carrying on with Abigail while I got ready and a group of other Peregrinos were gathered around chatting with us.

One of them, a muscular dude with an indistinguishable accent, said, laughing, a little darkly, "You're like all Americans."

"How so?" I asked?

"Because you're always like…" he said, and he made an invisible sock puppet with his right hand and, in a high falsetto, cried, "Blah blah blah blah" and laughed, along with everyone else, except Abigail.

It was said as a joke, but meant, in whole or in part, as an insult.

I laughingly replied, "Buen FUCKING Camino, Asshole!" and marched off, first to the nearby port-o-potty, then off to the ferry.

I was quite annoyed to be insulted like that, and feeling frustrated. Then I got to thinking, "well, maybe he's a quiet person. Who likes quiet people. And finds loud, always joking people like me annoying. Which is fine because I don't care for quiet people who don't talk or joke. So I wouldn't have cared for him. And he wouldn't have cared for me. So I don't care at all what he thought of me. And if he thought I was loud, well, fair play to him. But that's what I'm like, so I won't let him make me feel bad about it. I like it. Great."

And that was it. Abigail and I spoke briefly about it as we walked, and I think she was madder than I was. But after a moment, I let it go and we moved on to laughing and joking and chatting.

I can't really believe it was that easy. It felt, in that conversation I'd had with myself, like being Emil. Light, easy, unphased, fun. Easy. And that is a person whose shoes I never thought I'd get the opportunity to walk in.

Even Abigail was impressed. "You got over dat much faster dan I taught you would, eh? I really thought that was going to upset you for quite a while."

It felt good to let it (mostly) go. That could have been one of those moments I'd carry with me forever, and would replay time and again, editing the ending and reliving all of the emotions of the Blake it happened to. But it won't be. In a few days all the poison will be drained from that memory, and it will stand only as a testament to my growth, development, and acceptance and love of myself.

In Santander Abigail, Leo, and I had amazing tortilla and coffee, then carried on. Leo split off to (unsuccessfully) buy shoe inserts (the asphalt is KILLER on the soles of the feet) and Abigail and I continued on through Santander.

We had all said, after so many long days, that we would have a short day. The problem is, however, that sometimes you get to a city early in the day, or your get there hours before the albergue opens, or it just isn't a nice place and has nothing to keep you there. In all of these cases, the best thing is to keep walking. There's usually another place in 5 KM (3.11 mi.), which at first would have seemed impossible, but now we don't even think about it. If we arrive somewhere and it just doesn't feel right, we just keep going.

Yesterday, from Santander onward, the way was ugly. Ugly buildings, ugly highway, ugly Camino. So we just kept going.

I was losing my mind a bit, to be honest, between the asphalt and the uninteresting scenery, and the endless KM we were walking. But rather than complain, I just kept going and remembered, like it or not, I just had to keep going, so I may as well enjoy it. So I started singing, and playing games with myself, and enjoying mine and Abigail's company, rather than complain and shout and yell like I wanted to.

As Abigail said, "resistance makes it worse. Just accept what you have to do and do it in the best, most fun way you can."

The albergue was fantastic when we arrived, and we spent the night, Jacob, Isabella, Leo, Abigail, and myself laughing and chatting until we slept.

The Albergue had fresh, clean sheets which smelled like fabric softener, and fresh towels. It was amazing to sleep without our sleeping bags, and to dry off with a soft towel. How quickly we begin to immensely appreciate the smallest of things when we strip away all the niceties the modern world in which we live affords us. I didn't even know I liked drying off with a soft towel. The thought had never occurred to me.

All in all, it was another great day on the Camino, and one which felt

Day 10

hard won, and full of victories, particularly in that realm of uncertainty and instability between my ears.

All my lovin',

- Blake.

Pride

1. I'm proud that I was so quickly able to reset my mind after two moments of upset today.
2. I'm proud that Abigail and I pressed on and found a lovely albergue after some very ugly walking today.
3. I'm proud that I make Abigail, who is so funny, laugh with reckless abandon.

Gratitude

1. I'm grateful for the fresh clean sheets, and the free towel I've been given at this albergue.
2. I'm grateful for the excellent company I've had on the journey. No mood-hoovers.
3. I'm grateful for the friends I have at home in Berlin, who are always so excited to hear from me, and be with me.

Day 11

BOO DE PIÉLAGOS → CÓBRECES

35 km / 21.75 mi.

Thursday, August 31st, 2017

19:21

*N*othing much to report today. We're staying in an abbey...or what used to be the barn of the abbey. 30 beds in a city with 8 pilgrims! But we've been having a lovely evening.

Today was one of the hardest both physically and mentally. This morning was rain and industry. It was hard to stay positive and motivated, but I'm happy to report I was able to keep my spirits up and feet moving.

I think it's safe to say that I've moved into the part of the Camino where the challenge becomes mental. We still have 500 KM (310.69 mi.) to go, and while I love the walking, that's a very daunting reality. It's hard to stay motivated, especially in the ugly parts of the walk, like this morning.

Luckily, the second half was sunny, and the scenery was stupendous. We noticed the sights, architecture and scenery begin to change as we near the end of Cantabria and enter Asturias.

Jacob calculated that today would be 30 KM (18.64 mi.). It was exhausting and while Olivia and Isabella blasted ahead, I could hardly keep up with Jacob, who, though extremely fit, is 40 years my senior. I was wiped, I was so tired by the end, I nearly cried when we had to take a slightly roundabout way to get to the abbey in the last 30 meters, and

that's not an exaggeration. I could hardly contain the tears.

Turns out Jacob miscalculated. It was 35 KM (21.75 mi.), which we did in 6.5 hours. An average of 5.3 KM/hour (3.29 mi./hour).

Still, the way was mostly easy, and we've had longer days, so I must be getting worn down over time, and I DEFINITELY need to eat more.

Day 11

I'm burning far more calories than I'm taking in.

The evening was great, and the laughs and chats were capped off with a great meal and a bottle of wine I bought for us to celebrate our long day. We've now lost Leo, and Isabella will leave soon. Our little family is dwindling!

All my lovin',

-Blake

Pride

1. I'm proud I did 35 KM (21.75 mi.) today!
2. I'm proud I kept my mind calm and clear when I wanted to lse it this morning on an ugly camino, in the rain.
3. I'm proud that I haven't yet missed a day of journaling.

Gratitude

1. I'm grateful that the shower today was soooo hot.
2. I'm grateful that the Sun came out today and the second half of the way was fantastic.
3. I'm grateful that I have a be to sleep in tonight. I'm. So. tired.

Day 12

CÓBRECES → SERDIO

30 km / 18.64 mi.

Day 12

Friday, September 1st, 2017

16:29

Today was, in my opinion, the most beautiful section of the journey. The weather was sunny and cool all day. I watched a gorgeous sunrise over a beach from a hilltop. The entire day was spent on quiet roads going through tiny, beautiful, affluent pueblos nestled in the nooks and crannies of the hills, corn fields, copses of towering eucalyptus trees, tiny model towns with clay colored canopies, all bordered by the astounding Picos de Europa Mountains looming in the distance, and the emerald-teal Bay of Biscay.

Ironically, I took almost no photos on this magnificent day, but it was just too beautiful to attempt to capture. I felt it more appropriate just to sit, stare, and enjoy.

Physically, it was another very hard day in spite of the relatively short 30 KM (18.64 mi.) and the easy, rolling terrain. I was broken by the end of the day when we arrived at the albergue in Serdio, far more broken than my companions.

I spent most of the day contemplating another nightmare. Tour groups were descending upon my apartment, a lovely adobe cave, and taking their rest breaks there, snacking and chatting and lounging in my private abode.

The management had rented my space out for a few hours a day to tour groups in need of rest to earn money, and plead as I might, they wouldn't even schedule a meeting with me to discuss the arrangement. The invading tourists descended in endless waves.

That musician was there again. We chatted amicably. She was my neighbor. I upset her briefly somehow.

The rest of the day I was contemplating the dream, and what it made me feel. I don't think of dreams as premonitions or signs or even necessarily meaningful interpretations of the goings on of my subconscious. But, the dream itself made me feel things. First, sadness that I quit playing music, and that my dreams passed me by. Then, hope that music can still be a meaningful part of my life. Then pride at the improvements I made during the making of Bottle Up and Explode. Then desire to play, and excitement for the making of my next record, tentatively entitled A Tale of Love and Loss, which I'll begin working on directly upon my return to Berlin.

Lastly an urge to go see that musician play when I return to Berlin.

All my lovin',

- Blake.

Day 12

Pride

1. I am proud that I am speaking so openly and easily with everyone I'm meeting in the hostel, including a lovely Swedish girl.
2. I'm proud that I kept moving forward today and yesterday, even though I'm having new pains everywhere, all the time.
3. I'm proud that I so easily flirted with a girl I liked all night tonight.

Gratitude

1. I'm grateful that I've been convinced to do the Primitive Route
2. I'm grateful I could spend the evening with a girl I was interested in.
3. I'm grateful for this incredibly comfy bed I'm in tonight.

Day 13

SERDIO → LLANES

43 km / 26.72 mi

Saturday, September 2nd, 2017
16:37

*V*ery little to report today. The walking was, again, gorgeous. I walked alone most of the day, though I started out walking a bit with a very pretty, very friendly and sweet Swedish girl I met in our albergue last night. I admit I had a bit of a crush on her, and was quite flirty last night over drinks and this morning while we walked.

Still, I was in the mood to walk alone a bit, so I walked on. The weather was gorgeous, and the scenery was a delight, climbing high up into the hills before 9:00 for gorgeous panoramas of verdant, rolling countryside.

One thing of note: while I was so wrecked the last two days, today was physically maybe the best I felt! I really was going! We left Serdio a little around 7:30, and were in Cóbreces, 10 KM (6.21 mi.) away, by about 8:45, meaning I was walking about 6 KM (3.73 mi.)/hour without even trying!

In the end, we walked nearly 43 KM (26.72 mi.) today!

Llanes is a lovely city, and I spent the afternoon having beers on a hillside cafe with Abigail overlooking the quaint beach and the roofs of the city, before having a swim and a delicious feast with Abigail and Jacob.

Today was one of the best on the Camino.

All my lovin',

- Blake.

Day 13

Pride

1. I'm proud that we walked <u>43 KM</u> (<u>26.72 mi.</u>) today, and I feel tired, but great! Bring on the <u>Primitivo</u>!
2. I'm proud that I didn't get furious with myself when I got lost two times. I used the 3 P's and was okay!
3. I'm proud that I so thoroughly enjoyed my time walking alone today, and even chose it over walking with the very pretty, very sweet Ashley from Sweden.

Gratitude

1. I'm grateful for the gorgeous weather, and the incredible views, and amazing walk today.
2. I'm grateful for the health of my body, which carried me 43 KM (26.72 mi.), and I feel fine.
3. I'm grateful that after an excellent day of walking, I have a lovely, white sand, crystal clear water beach to relax on.

Day 14

LLANES → RIBADESELLA

35 km / 21.75 mi.

What started out as a luxurious, slow start with breakfast in our hotel at 8:00, and hitting the road at 8:30, coupled with a lovely walk along a coast full of serene beaches, slowly devolved into the hardest moment of my Camino.

Slowly but surely the idyllic scenery gave way to asphalt, highway, and uninteresting urban sprawl.

While there were a few poignant moments, such as the abandoned monastery in a corn field which I got to explore, overall the day felt like a long, drawn out slog through hot, grey weather.

My mind felt heavy and uneasy, perhaps brought on by the fact that today marked the halfway point, over 400 KM (248.55 mi.), and that left me both worried that I'm walking the Camino too quickly, and nervous about what I'll feel when it's all over.

I was able to combat the weight of my thoughts for the last six draining KM by singing and practicing silly runs with my voice, but when I got to my albergue I found out that Isabella was in a farther city, Abigail stopped in a previous one, Jacob was in a different hotel, and I was going to pay 20 EUR for an albergue which was more a surf school,

leaving me feeling very much out of place and alone.

That they asked me to leave my bag in a garage downstairs and take to my room the things I needed in a plastic garbage sack deepened my sense of vagrant waywardness and was as demoralizing as it was dehumanizing and irritating. Having so little in my bag to begin with, I essentially NEED everything in it, so I basically repacked everything into a trash bag.

It was all I could do to hold back the tears, which were pressing desperately on the backs of my eyelids, but I wasn't able to explain why.

I went directly to the beach. Swimming in the sea always feels quite cleansing.

I swam in the water for a few brief moments when the tears began to flow. It was perhaps the first moment I felt alone enough to cry. There was no one in the water.

"This is good," I thought. "Let it out." Out came a mighty sob. One, two, and just before the third erupted, the loudspeakers cut on. In Spanish echoed a voice.

"You in the blue swimsuit. You are swimming in a NO SWIM zone. Please exit the water immediately! I repeat: Exit the water immediately!"

So, cursing the beach, the city, the albergue, and all of Spain, I stomped out of the water and went to shower, my tears choked back, but unattended.

I met with Jacob for a few very teary beers before dinner. I was feeling so inexplicably emotional and it was all I could do the whole time to keep from crying.

Dinner was excellent, and before going to bed I called Jennifer, which made me feel better. It's always good to talk to people you love, who love you right back.

Jacob and I planned to walk the next stage to Sebrayo in two parts: 18 KM (11.19 mi.) to Las Isla and 14 KM (8.7 mi.) to Sebrayo in order to meet with Olivia before heading to the Primitivo, and to give our legs a rest before heading to the mountainous terrain ahead.

All my lovin',

— Blake.

Day 14

Pride

1. I am proud that I am in such good physical shape.
2. I am proud that I'm easily able to express my emotions.
3. I am proud that I am writing in my journal daily.

Gratitude

1. I am grateful that I was able to swim in the ocean after a long day.
2. I am grateful that I had such a delicious dinner with Jacob.
3. I am grateful that I was able to sleep with a blanket, and not use my sleeping bag.

Day 15

RIBADESELLA → LA ISLA

18 km / 11.18 mi.

oday was a short and VERY sweet walk. The entirety of the 18 KM (11.18 mi.) was in green woods, through tiny, quaint villages, and along the verdant hills of the coast, with some of the best views we've had so far.

La Isla is a tiny city, but beautiful, and the Albergue here is, surprisingly, packed. It's not a place I figure many would stop, as I'm certain it isn't on an end point in any guide, but I suppose it's just the right distance from the other nice places to make it a common stopping point.

While I had hoped Abigail, who stopped 6 KM (3.73 mi.) before us yesterday would be happy to stop here for a very normal 24 KM (14.91 mi.), it turns out she's blown past us on an almost 36 KM (22.37 mi.) day for her.

It made me really sad, to be honest. Isabella, too, has departed from our little crew, meaning that all that is left if Jacob and I don't meet with Olivia tomorrow, will be me and Jacob, with the other people whom I've most enjoyed on either side of us, spread throughout the Camino.

While I'm happy to modify my pace to keep my little group together, the same can't be said of everyone, of course! The Camino is a deeply

personal experience, and the pace at which one walks it is part of that experience.

Connecting with the people around me is one of the most important things in my life, and because I find true connection to be quite hard to find, when I find it, I throw myself head first. I become very quickly attached to the people with whom I feel a connection, and while I think it is a beautiful quality, it is also very difficult for me to let people go, and if I'm not careful, having that connection severed can sometimes feel very personal.

I don't believe we'll now be able to catch Abigail, and that really upsets me because I really felt a connection with her. While I fully respect her need to continue on, her presence will be missed terribly, especially for all the laughter she brought.

I just get too attached too quickly, and I think goodbyes carry with them some sense of abandonment issues, probably brought on by a period of my childhood in which I lived with neither of my parents at an age when I would have been far too young to understand it. However, I don't think it dawned on me until today, when Abigail went ahead, that the feeling of abandonment is far more wrapped up with goodbyes and farewells, and probably partly causes my need for, love of, and propensity for attaching myself to others so quickly.

While I don't want to be more guarded in my attachments, nor less touched by life, it is fundamental that I learn to seperate goodbyes from this deep, powerful yearning dread I feel at their exit; that I learn to distinguish between the inevitable moment someone takes their natural and timely leave from my life, and the sense of abandonment that so often accompanies it. I hate goodbyes.

And I've lived long enough and said goodbye to enough people to know just how final "goodbye" so often is.

The halfway point of the Camino is marked with pensiveness, sadness, and fear for that day in 400 KM (248.55 mi.) time when it's all over and I have to return from it.

I am still thoroughly enjoying the experience, but I must admit I am emotional in a way I did not expect to be.

Time to open myself back up, and continue meeting lovely new people, which is of course the aim of this journey.

Today is the last day we will see the sea before coming to Fennesterre. I am happy to have chosen La Isla for our stopping point. I got to swim one last time in the Bay of Biscay, and have enjoyed the lapping of waves upon the shore while I wrote this entry, which was appropriately all about saying goodbye.

Saddened though I am by my departure from the sea, I am excited about the change of pace the Primitivo's Path into the mountains, away from the asphalt and industry, will bring.

All my lovin',

- Blake

Day 15

Pride

1. I am proud to have made it halfway (over 400 **KM** / 248.55 mi.) to Santiago.
2. I am proud I am using journaling as a means of understanding my thoughts and feelings, and calming my mind.
3. I am proud that I love deeply and genuinely, even when it is sometimes painful to do so.

Gratitude

1. I am grateful for the wonderful shower I had today.
2. I am grateful for the chance to say goodbye to the Ocean.
3. I am grateful to have met so many lovely, interesting people on the Camino.

Day 16

LA ISLA → LA VEGA DE SERIEGO

43 KM / 26.72 mi.

Tuesday, September 5th, 2017

18:35

oday was full of lessons...or rather today there was a single occurrence which taught me many lessons.

After a fully sleepless night in which I tried futilely to saw a few logs between the deafening snores, the sensation (pathologic though it may have been) of bed bugs crawling on me, and the stressful thoughts of coordinating meetup up with Olivia, Jacob and I were on the road before 6:30.

We stopped for coffee, but were in Sebrayo, a mere 14 KM (8.7 mi.) away from La Isla, by 10:15. The albergue didn't open until 15:00, and Olivia wouldn't be there until far later. Abigail was there the night before, and would be long gone, and Jacob was going to keep moving as well.

I'd spent the morning debating what to do. Go back on my word and continue down the road, which is certainly what I wanted to do, or Stay and wait for Olivia, but lose a day waiting in a village so small it doesn't have even a store in it, and risk not seeing Abigail or Jacob again.

I was torn, but in the end, my gut knew what was right, and I knew I had to follow it. I texted Olivia and apologized profusely, and told her I

was sorry, but I had to keep moving. I felt terrible, but I knew it was the right thing to do.

I feel there was so much to learn from this small experience. It says a lot about myself, and for brevity's sake, I'll just list them.

1. For me, the most important thing in life is personal connection. I'll sacrifice quite a lot to create, facilitate, and keep personal connections alive, even when it is detrimental to what I actually want.

2. I should make sure to listen to my gut/heart/instinct even when it's hard, and even when doing so might upset others. Olivia may have been upset that I kept going, but she'll have understood, and it really was the right thing for me. I felt that relief immediately.

3. **I spend far too much time looking back, and too little time looking forward.** I'm super prone to nostalgia, and that's okay as long as it doesn't impede my life. I, however, am so prone to

nostalgia that I spend too much time nursing relationships and fantasies of the past instead of looking to be excited by and creating new ones.

If I wanted to reconnect with Olivia, it's because there is a sense that there isn't a connection just as nice to be had at the next albergue. Looking back blinds me to the things on the horizon, and often precludes me from enjoying new fulfilling experiences waiting just around the bend.

This is true of friendships, jobs, relationships, experiences, everything. I must learn to appreciate the past, enjoy that nostalgia, but without letting it direct my life.

Jacob and I walked another 43 KM (26.72 mi.), began the Primitivo, and made it to an albergue in La Vega, where a smiling Abigail greeted us from the second story window of the little house, laughing about how she knew it was us because she recognized the *click-clack* of Jacob's walking sticks.

I was thrilled to see her.

Tomorrow, we're off to Oviedo, an easy 26 KM, where the primitivo officially begins.

All my lovin',

- Blake.

Pride

1. I'm proud that I easily walked 43 KM (26.72 mi.) on no sleep, and feel fine!
2. I'm proud that I continued walking today, even though it was hard to tell Olivia I couldn't wait for her, and I felt bad about it.
3. I'm proud that although I was sad today about not stopping to meet Olivia, I found a way to stay calm and learn some lessons from it.

Gratitude

1. I'm grateful that Jacob and I have the same pace and attitude toward walking.
2. I'm grateful that the first day of the Primitivo was so primitivo, off the asphalt, and beautiful.
3. I'm grateful that Abigail happened to be at the same Albergue that Jacob and I stopped at today.

Day 17

LA VEGA DE SERIEGO → OVIEDO

26 km / 16.16 mi.

*V*ery little to report on the scenery front today. While the morning was quiet and pretty, the mist pouring out of the trees, and little aside from the clicks of my walking sticks and the hollow thud of my footsteps on the damp ground for a soundtrack, the rest of the morning was spent walking on asphalt through uninteresting urban sprawl and horrifying industry.

Central Oviedo, old town is quite nice, but the rest of the city is nothing to write home about.

In the silence of the morning walk, my brain turned to all the things I have to do when I get home. Visa, jobs, lawyer, therapy, etc.

I was instantly covered in a cold sweat, my heart racing

"Oh, hello, anxiety," I said aloud. "Haven't seen you in a while."

I tried to remind myself that while we are on the tail end of the trip, it isn't over yet, and I have no reason to think of all these things. Not yet. But that didn't work.

Finally, it was a phrase uttered last night by Elizabeth, a 25 year old, very sweet French woman wise beyond her years, which cut the anxiety to the quick.

"Toutes est faisable," I said aloud, and suddenly my body began returning to stasis.

"Everything is doable." Simple, ineloquent, but concise, and true.

Not to mention that the offhand, blasé way it sounds in French really helps hammer home the silliness of worrying about it all.

Give something a try. If it doesn't work out, who cares? Nothing bad will happen. Just gather yourself and try something else.

A new motto.

A safety net. A new reminder of the simplicity of it all.

Toutes est faisable.

All my lovin',

- Blake.

Day 17

Pride

1. I'm proud that I shut my anxiety down today.
2. I'm proud that I had such a productive afternoon after walking 26 KM
3. I'm proud that I stayed positive while walking through some very ugly scenery today.

Gratitude

1. I'm grateful that my home doesn't have bed bugs.
2. I'm grateful that I have money for dinner and new clothes to spend €12 at the laundromat
3. I'm grateful I am privileged enough to be on the Camino and have the time, energy, and money for this trip.

Day 18

OVIEDO → SAN JUAN DE VILLA PAÑADA

30 KM / 18.64 mi.

Thursday, September 7th, 2017

20:50

Today was wonderful although I started the day with a feeling of being a bit fed up with hostel life.

When the ambiance in the albergue is one of individualism and isolation, it makes sharing the tiny space together very unpleasant. It feels as though everyone is intruding on your space.

I was telling Abigail this morning as we walked from the city into the countryside that I had this feeling in all the albergues since Serdio. I've been disappointed since Bilbao, when all the Spaniards went home from the Camino.

She reminded me that all emotions are a wave, good and bad. Being tired of the Albergue life this morning is not a sign that I'll always be tired of it, just that I was tired of it this morning. And how right she was.

I was in need of a good albergue experience, and this is exactly what we got today.

We walked 30 KM (18.64 mi.) to an albergue in a tiny place, so tiny there are no shops or stores or anything apart from the church, a few houses, and their farm animals.

Sitting high in the hills, the tiny, very cozy albergue with amazing showers has a garden with a wonderful view of the green hills, and the city of Grado nestled in the nook of the hills. Lambs and donkeys and dogs make a soundtrack for the evening.

22 beds, 23 people, everyone kind and sociable and friendly. Everyone chatting and making friends. It was exactly what I needed.

The Camino always seems to give you what you want, right when you need it.

Day 18

Abigail and I made pasta and ate together, and the evening was spent enjoying everyone's company and playing a baby guitar.

I'm so pleased to be on the Camino.

All my lovin',

- Blake.

Pride

1. I'm proud that Abigail wants to call me Blake runner, because I'm so fast.
2. I'm proud that Germans are speaking to me in German.
3. I'm proud that Abigail liked the past I cooked tonight.

Gratitude

1. I'm grateful that today was such a wonderful walk.
2. I'm grateful that the woman at the grocery store trusted me to donate €5.00 in Santiago.
3. I'm grateful that I have so many lovely people to send videos and messages to.

Day 19

SAN JUAN DE VILLA PAÑADA → BODENAYA

25 km / 15.53 mi.

Thursday, September 8th, 2017

17:01

Today was perhaps...is almost certainly...the best day on the Camino.

After yet another essentially sleepless night (I long ago gave up the notion of getting sleep on the Camino) I finally slept around 5:30. I didn't awake until 7:30, and the albergue was half-empty. Having reserved my place in the albergue of Bodenaya, 25 KM (15.53 mi.) away, I didn't need to worry about hurrying. I decided that today would be a day dedicated to taking my sweet time.

I left around 9:00, and arrived at the albergue around 16:00, still one of the first. I really enjoy going fast, apparently much faster than most other pilgrims.

I enjoyed every step of the 25 KM (15.53 mi.) today. The scenery was magnificent and varied, from tiny pueblos to narrow valleys; from forest trials with foliage canopies next to babbling streams to hillside views of everything I'd walked. The Sun was bright, the breezes cool, and the temperature perfect. Almost all of today was offroad and completely alone. I spent my time stopping to enjoy it all, and coming up with a birthday song for my mom, whose birthday is today. I recorded it on a

hilltop and sent it to her before arriving at the albergue.

Internally, everything was close to perfect as well. I awoke with joy in my heart, the result of a delightful dream in which I was reunited with my ex-girlfriend, Carolina, for a fantastic night of love and laughter, and kissing so vivid it gave me butterflies thinking about it later.

The rest of the day, like yesterday, I felt like I was in love. That warm, cozy, Sunday morning, coffee with a long-time lover type of love, far from overwhelming, but all-encompassing just the same.

I was thrilled to be alone. I passed up several lovely people from last night's albergue in lieu of being alone. It was wonderful. As it turns out, I'm great company!

Interestingly, today I found myself thinking about Sophia, and replaying some of the things that happened while we were together that I didn't like. My therapist tried pointing out a pattern of her disrespecting me, and me not seeing it as disrespect. Even then I wasn't sure what he was talking about. But today I saw what he was talking about. Today I could clearly see that pattern. It's another sign of how far I've come, and how I've learned to value myself. The lack of that value caused my blindness.

I don't mind. I love her still, and hold nothing against her. That I see now the ways in which she disrespected me is simply because I value myself now more than I did when we were together. And I'm thrilled to know I've come far enough to see it.

All my lovin',

— Blake.

Pride

1. I'm proud that I enjoyed being alone all day today.
2. I'm proud that people applauded when I played guitar and sang.
3. I'm proud that I had my best day on the Camino.

Gratitude

1. I'm grateful that today was a perfect Camino day.
2. I'm grateful that Gavin had a guitar I could play.
3. I'm grateful that the albergue is so wonderful and comfortable and cozy.

Day 20

BODENAYA → CAMPIELLO

25 KM / 15.53 mi

Today was hands down the best day I've had on the Camino. It was wonderful from start to finish.

The day began with a communal breakfast. At dinner the night before we collectively decided to awake at 6:50. Gavin woke the entire albergue at exactly 6:50 with the smell of coffee, and the beautiful, peaceful "Ave Maria." that was my Grandfather's favorite song, and it felt so warm and peaceful to start the day with thoughts and memories of him filling my heart and head.

The coffee was excellent and plentiful, and the nutella was a very welcome change of pace in terms of condiments for the thick, hearty wheat bread we were served. Everyone at the table was smiling ,and the feeling was very cozy and familiar. I took my time and slowly got ready, chatting with the friendly pilgrims I had met. Upon leaving, hugs were exchanged. If there's one thing I have missed on the Camino, it's physical contact.

The walking was excellent. Stunning views, and plenty of solitude and silence to enjoy them. Even the heavy rain in the morning was a nice

change of pace. Eventually the Sun came out, revealing the splendor of the hills and lighting the forests I walked through. A beautiful, cold Fall breeze caressed my face, an appropriate metaphor for the change of season occurring all around, and all within me.

In the early afternoon, just after the Sun came out, I came across a pylon in the forest with a scallop shell pointing the way. Under it, someone had sloppily spray painted "228 KM (141.67 mi.)," I assumed a reference to the distance remaining to Santiago. The first time I saw such a reference was on Day 2 of El Camino, between San Sebastián and Deba. It said, "Santiago 787 KM (489.02 mi.)."

"Wow, Blake," I said jovially, aloud. "Look how far you've come!"

Suddenly, and without warning, a wave of intense emotion washed over me, and as I stared out through a clearing in the trees along the trail upon the sprawling green hills awash in the afternoon Sun, I burst into tears; tears that were neither of joy nor of sorrow, but rather of recognition. Indeed, I was sobbing for the nearly 600 KM (327.82 mi.) I had walked on the Camino, which I genuinely feared I would be unable to finish. But I was also sobbing for the distance I had traveled on my own personal Camino over the last 12 months. In June I felt suicidal. Now, I feel it is impossible that I'll ever find myself so lost, so hopeless, so utterly finished with life. Nothing is certain, but I feel this with the same certainty with which I am certain that I'll have the pleasure of waking up tomorrow, and the joy of falling truly and deeply in love.

Wow, Blake. Look how far you've come. Farther than you've ever believed possible. Farther than you ever could have hoped. And the journey is far from over.

The rest of the journey was peaceful and even included a stroll through an abandoned monastery, once an obligatory stop for every pilgrim, now in ruins.

The albergue was comfortable, and the pilgrim menu delicious and plentiful.

And, as if all that wasn't enough, who should walk through the albergue door but Olivia, who had walked nearly 40 KM (24.85 mi.) because the albergue in Bodenaya was closed. I was simply overjoyed.

Tomorrow is meant to be one of the hardest stages of all the Caminos, with a massive 1,000 meter (3,280 feet) ascent, and 16.5 KM (10.25 mi.) hiking through the hillside with no resources of any kind. I'm incredibly excited.

All my lovin',

- Blake.

Day 20

Pride

1. I'm so proud I've come this far down the Camino
2. I'm proud I bought Olivia a tiny gift as a gesture to show I'm sorry about not seeing her.
3. I'm proud that I stayed calm and enjoyed dinner with a bunch of strangers when I felt myself getting stressed about it.

Gratitude

1. I'm grateful for the Camino's message that I can complete it, and the weight it carried with it.
2. I'm grateful for all the excellent pilgrim service we got in the albergue and restaurant/shop.
3. I'm grateful for another fantastic day on the Camino.
4. I'm grateful Olivia caught us!

Day 21

CAMPIELLO → BERDUCEDO

27 KM / 16.78 mi.

The walk today was splendid, filled with breathtaking panoramas from the tops of massive hillsides.

I spent the entire walk alone, enjoying the scenery, the solitude, and the cows and horses that wandered freely through the hillside munching on the grass.

In my walk I thought a while about Olivia. The natural people pleaser in me was unsatisfied with the interaction we had the night before. Although I was thrilled to see her, I felt a distance from her. Admittedly, it could be completely of my own imagination or a projection of my insecurities, or real, but caused by something completely unrelated. However, her steadfast rejection of a tiny pin I bought, along with a round of beers as a gesture of how sorry I was left me feeling unpardoned, my guilt unsquelched. So, I thought about it, and went down the normal path of feeling bad, guilty, and desperate to make it up to her. The people pleaser in me was running wild. I was ready to do what I always do: define myself based on the beliefs and perceptions of others; to dislike myself equally as much as I assume those around me dislike me. Come to think of it, I only realized this is something I do on

the walk this morning.

Upon realizing this, I stopped and tried to imagine what she might think about me, and how this reflected against how I feel about myself and how I handled the situation. The two didn't add up. Perhaps more importantly, I felt confident in how I felt about the situation, and how I handled it, and that was regardless of however she might feel about all of it.

> <u>That is to say:</u> How she felt has absolutely no impact on how I felt, and what I knew. The two things existed independently of each other. <u>One didn't impact the other!</u>

This was quite a realization for me. How I feel about myself and my actions necessarily exists independently of the ideas, feelings, and opinions of others. I can feel about myself what and how I want regardless of what others think and feel about me. I must.

And I felt better. Much better. It was a very liberating realization. While

I will need lots of time and practice breaking the habit of allowing my opinions of myself to mirror those I presume others have of me, knowing that it's possible, knowing that I can, fills me with hope and self love.

Another powerful realization today: My sister truly and genuinely loves me.

Because I'm so much older than her, and moved out of the house when she was ten and never really came back, we've spent relatively little time together. And so today, I realized that when she says, "I love you," it isn't the American "Love" as in, "I love popcorn," or "I love my new toothpaste." It's the love of one sibling to another, who share common ties and experiences. The relatively little time we've spent together doesn't negate the time and experiences we have had together, and her love for me is the same as my love for her. Unconditional and deep. And I feel so lucky for it.

I think I'll have a few too many drinks tonight, just to ensure a few solid hours of unconsciousness. While sleep and I have always had a troubled relationship, and while I've come to terms with the insomnia which has plagued me on the Camino, last night's sleeplessness really got to me. I just want, need, a night of unconsciousness.

All my lovin',

- Blake.

Day 21

Pride

1. I'm proud I so easily walked this stage of El Camino, meant to be one of the hardest of any Camino.
2. I'm proud that I'm learning to learn from my mistakes and let them slide.
3. I'm proud that I had a very pleasant dinner with total strangers.

Gratitude

1. I'm grateful for the good weather we had on the walk today.
2. I'm grateful for the clean bed and personal shelf I had in the albergue
3. I'm grateful for the good company I had all evening.

Day 22

BERDUCEDO → GRANDE DE SALIME

20 KM / 12.43 mi.

oday was short and sweet.

Although I spent most of the morning with a minor hangover, it was well worth it for the laughs I had, and the 7 hours of uninterrupted unconsciousness I had last night. Of course, I was tired today because drunk sleep is always unsatisfying, unproductive sleep, but at the very least I didn't spend all night lying awake waiting for sleep that would never come. It was bliss.

After a slow start and two coffees with Abigail, we set to walking. It was a wonderful walk through forests with excellent views and a nice temperature.

I think today I experienced the closest thing to pure calm, zen-buddhist happiness I've ever felt. I was walking along and felt a moment of utter contentment. I wanted nothing. I missed nothing. I needed nothing. I thought nothing. I felt almost empty, but in a really positive, pleasant, calm way. The walking was exactly what I wanted/needed. I felt I was exactly where I should be doing exactly what I should be doing.

Nothing was missing, and nothing could be taken away.

It was as close to perfection as any moment I have ever had.

Tonight at the albergue we cooked together and enjoyed some delicious wine and some good conversation.

The kitchen here is so good and so well equipped that I've decided to take our time and make breakfast tomorrow morning.

I'm making breakfast tacos, and I can't wait. We're all very excited for a proper breakfast, something Spaniards seem to know nothing about.

All my lovin',

— Blake.

Day 22

Pride

1. I'm proud that Kyle found a use for all of our conversation today.
2. I'm proud that I'm open, honest, and vulnerable.
3. I'm proud that I was so calm and relaxed around Olivia, even with the thought that she might be upset at me.

Gratitude

1. I'm grateful that Kyle made us dinner.
2. I'm grateful that the Sun shined, and the walk was gorgeous.
3. I'm grateful that I was unconscious for seven solid hours last night.

Day 23

GRANDAS DE SALIME → A FONSAGRADA

27 KM / 16.78 mi.

Tuesday, September 12th, 2017

no time recorded

*L*ast night was the first real, solid, un-alcohol induced night of sleep I have had on the Camino, and while I still feel a bone-deep exhaustion, the result of intense physical exertion and an accumulation of dozens of hours of lost sleep, I was so grateful for the sleep, and the strange, intense dreams it bestowed upon me.

I awoke at 6:40 and immediately began cooking breakfast tacos in the kitchen. I was so happy for the tiny taste of normalcy, of my everyday life, the act of making breakfast provided.

The tacos were delicious, and I was thrilled to fill everyone's bellies with something other than white bread and sugary cookies.

After a quick cup of coffee at the bar, I set off into the rain where I blasted through an easy, if uneventful 27 KM (16.78 mi.). The weather was a mixture of wind and rain and fog and clouds, reducing what would otherwise have been stunning views to a wall of grey 20 feet from my face in every direction.

Still, the rain was kind of a fun change of pace, and at least removed any need to stop for photos. So I walked and enjoyed the exercise, the time alone, and the occasional chat with the friendly pilgrims I passed up.

As I walked today I thought about the end of my trip which is approaching rapidly.

"Ooof…" I said aloud, "I'm a bit scared to go home…"

Then I thought about that. Why are you scared to go home?

"Because I have some things I need to take care of…visa…etc."

"Yeah, but you'll take care of it. No problem. And if it doesn't work out the way you thought or hoped it would, you'll find a way to make things work."

"Oh yeah…"

"Yeah! You know you can do anything…and if you can't , you'll try something else."

"Oh yeah…"

"Easy. There's nothing bad that can happen. Nothing. There's nothing to be afraid of. There's nothing to fear. Toutes est faisable."

"Oh yeah…It's only the fear that causes the problems…my fear…that causes the anxiety…but there's nothing to be afraid of…Because nothing bad can happen…and even when things don't work out as planned, there's always something else that I can do…something else that will happen…

"Truly, I have nothing to fear but fear itself…"

And I smiled and continued my walk.

If that's not a breakthrough, I don't know what is.

Today I had a wonderful lunch with Abigail and Olivia, and we had a really lovely time.

Another wonderful day on the Camino.

Another communal dinner, and another communal breakfast awaits.

All my lovin',

- Blake.

Pride

1. I'm proud that I am learning to conquer fear itself.
2. I'm proud that I walked so hard and so fast today.
3. I'm proud of the shape I'm in and the way my body looks.

Gratitude

1. I'm grateful for all the help my therapist has given me.
2. I'm grateful for the delicious pilgrim menu I had with Abigail and Olivia.
3. I'm grateful I got to eat a nice lunch with Olivia and the vibe was fun and lovely.

Day 24

A FONSAGRADA → CASTROVERDE

32 km / 19.88 mi.

Day 24

Wednesday, September 13th, 2017
4:17

Yet another night of insomnia on the Camino has led me to
writing in my journal at 4:00 AM in the hope that sleep might
come to relieve me of my consciousness afterward. I'd say I'm
annoyed, but at this point the sleeplessness has become a default, and at
least this way I won't have to write two journal entries later today.

Today was an excellent walk, mostly spent alone walking through
forests shrouded in mist and fog in the morning, and bathed in leaf
filtered sunlight in the afternoon.

The Primitivo has been a wonderful change of pace from the Norte.
The vibe and the people and the family feeling much more what I was
hoping to find.

Part of that vibe is a peacefulness in the Pilgrims. No one is waking
at 5:00 AM to run to the next albergue to queue up and wait outside
for a bed.

My little crew has been taking our sweet time, eating together and
having coffee and getting on the road around 9:00 AM.

This morning we had a pancake breakfast at the albergue and a fantastic

cup of coffee at a tidy little cafe before heading out at 9:00 AM.

Abigail, Olivia, and I had already passed the lion's share of our fellow pilgrims by the time we stopped for coffee at 11:15. I never worry about getting a bed anymore. I'm always among the first to arrive, and have more than once been called Speedy Gonzales.

Today I got to thinking about the Camino. Part of what makes it so enjoyable, so meditative, is the utter simplicity of it all. It's nearly impossible to get stressed, or angry, or upset when you know that the day ahead will literally be a walk in the park. Even my insomnia, which would normally drive me insane with frustration and worry, is only a minor irritation. I may be dog tired to the core of my bones, but it will hardly impede the walking.

I wondered how that simplicity differs from normal life, and slowly began to realize that the Camino, for all its simplicity, is deceptively similar to everyday life.

The fact that every day is a walk in the park doesn't mean it is easy. 43K up and down hills in the rain and heat and wind is difficult no matter how slowly you do it, or how well trained and prepared you are. But it's delightful.

And while I choose to walk the Camino, there is no shortage of events and occurrences of varying levels of severity and inconvenience which are completely outside of my control: the snoring Pilgrims keeping me awake, pouring rain, injuries of varying degrees of severity, bed bugs attacking me night after night, a desert of cafes, restaurants, supermarkets and water fountains for kilometers in all directions, unpleasant pilgrims, pouring rain, blazing Sun, closed albergues, full albergues, no beds to sleep in, insomnia, discomfort, illness, etc., etc., etc.

Still, all of these challenges do not seem to detract from the general joy and enjoyment I find on the Camino. I believe the reason for that is that in all of the simplicity of this journey, it is easy to see that while I may not be in control of any number of outside factors which I may encounter along the Camino, I am ALWAYS in control of how I react to those things which are outside of my control, and the power of that realization is intoxicating.

This is the mindset that I would like to come home with.

Because even in my "normal life," if I am truly living a life well lived, then every day is just another day on the Camino; every day is just a walk in the park. And like the Camino, some days will be inherently easier than others; some longer, some with greater distances to travel, more ups and downs, fewer resources or places to resupply, more isolated, more crowded, more beautiful, more challenging, more varied, less obviously interesting than others. But they are nevertheless just another day on the wonderful Camino

And like on the Camino, any number of things will happen to me, and all around me, which are completely out of my control. But, just like on the Camino, I am absolutely in control of how I react to those things, adapt to those things, and choose to move on from those things. I am always in control of choosing a new Camino which suits me more, and fulfills me more, and takes me away from those outside factors, or brings me toward wonderful new things & wonderful new, joyful occurrences (which are ALSO completely out of my control! It is so important to remember that many of the things which happen to us on our Caminos over which we have no control are also wonderful things: Rainbows, sunshine, a flock of lambs crossing our path, a new, interesting person talking to us, a free cup of coffee from a friendly bar man, a fountain appearing when our bottle is empty, falling in love, etc., etc., etc., etc.

I am brought to tears by the joy, and the hope, and empowerment with which this mindset fills me, and I am so grateful for yet another lesson this Camino has imparted upon me.

Day 24

It's now 5:15. I shall sneak back to my bunk, and if I'm lucky I'll be able to squeeze in another hour and a half of sleep before the room slowly fills with the sounds of stirring pilgrims and rustling bags.

And if not...no matter. Today is just another walk in the park.

All my lovin',

- Blake.

Pride

1. I'm proud I ran up steep hills today.
2. I'm proud I'm getting so much out of the Camino.
3. I'm proud I was the guide and got everyone a very nice dinner tonight.

Gratitude

1. I'm grateful for the privilege of being on the Camino.
2. I'm grateful for the excellent company I've had on the Camino.
3. I'm grateful for my excellent physical health.

Day 25

CASTROVERDE → LUGO

25 km / 15.53 mi.

When our guide book mentioned that the albergue in Castroverde was "new and modern," it neglected to mention that by "modern," it meant, "The albergue has done away with the need of a hospitalero being on duty in the morning by installing automatic, floodlight grade fluorescent lighting which switches on at 6:45, stripping all 34 sleeping pilgrims of their autonomy and adulthood by blinding them into wakefulness and submission until they get up against their will and leave the albergue."

So, though I was fortunate enough to get a bit of strange dream-laden sleep, the sweet blackness of unconsciousness was ripped away from me and all the other pilgrims, for, surprisingly, almost no one had arisen, cruelly, abruptly, and about 2 hours before I would have liked.

Still, all I had to do today was go for a walk, so after 50 pushups to get the blood flowing, Kyle, Abigail, Olivia, and I enjoyed a makeshift meal of muesli, fruit, and canned beans riddled with the delusional laughter and deranged silliness our sleep deprived states incited in us.

After a coffee in the city, we hit the road, where the Sun greeted us, along with hints of the coming fall: leaves scattered across the path, a cool breeze and lower hanging Sun, a hint of yellow in the forest canopy, and a shade of blue in the morning light.

The way was a mere 24 KM (14.91 mi.), and almost entirely flat as it wound through quiet forests and sleepy medieval towns, stone structures rising out of the ground, tucked away and unheard of for centuries, still secrets to the bustling modern world surrounding them. In spite of the ease of the walk itself, the persistent and prolonged nocturnal activity of my busy mind left me feeling drained, like a member of the walking dead, a shell of a man driven forward by an unknown external force.

The mind-body connection has never been so obvious. My body, trained, fit, and ready for action, seemed unable to move, and was quickly slowed and stiff, as if the gears were gummed up by a thick molasses of sleepiness floating freely throughout my body. The body was willing, but the spirit was weak. It was just as well that today was a short day.

After crossing through the Roman city of Lugo, which boasts the longest unbroken Roman city walls in the world (2 KM / 1.24 mi.), Olivia asked, on the home stretch to our hostel, "What kind of work will you look for when you're back in Berlin?"

I paused. After a moment, I calmly responded, "To be honest, I'm going to stay unemployed for a while." Relief. I elaborated, but the long and short of it is, once I get my Visa, and I WILL get my visa, I'm going to live on unemployment benefits for a while. I have over €1,200.00 per month coming in every month until next June, 2018. That's enough to live on in Berlin. I'm going to enjoy my time, open myself to any number of new opportunities, and fill my days practicing and recording my 2 EPs, and seeing what new exciting opportunities life brings.

The calmness and certainty and excitement with which I spoke of this plan really surprised me. Three months ago, I said the same thing, but with all the security and tranquility of a man living under a mountain of debt, and whose pants are currently on fire.

There is a calm, a comfort, I have begun to feel. Unburdened by the yoke of fear and anxiety which I have borne all my life, I am now beginning to see and feel all the possibilities that lie before me, and am excited by the prospect of choosing only the ones I want, not the ones I feel I SHOULD choose for whatever inane reasons I feel I should choose them, as much as I am enlivened by this unfamiliar confidence in the making of those decisions.

It seems beyond clear to me that living on my unemployment while focusing on music, and making myself available to new, unthought of opportunities to which my fears have blinded me, is precisely what I want to, need to, will do. I feel impervious to the scrutiny or judgement of others. This is MY Camino, and it is mine to walk precisely how I see fit. So that's just what I intend to do.

One of my hopes for the Camino was that it would give me time to think about what my guru, Dr. Tal Ben-Shahar, refers to as a guiding star, a sort of life-mission statement against which you can measure yourself, and which, like the stars, you can use to orient yourself to ensure that the path of your life is on course. If it isn't, you can use this guiding star to help steer your decision making to get yourself back on course.

("On Course" simply denotes that one is living in a way that honors and fulfills this life-mission statement, but acknowledges as well that there are any number of courses from all different directions which lead that way. It is not to imply that there is a single course which can meet the requirements of that statement.)

I believe I have come up with a rough draft for mine. It will probably need to be revised and refined, and one day it may be invalid and need to be completely rewritten. But I believe I have found a life-mission statement, a guiding star, which will serve me well in this change of seasons, in this personal revolution I find myself in the midst of.

> I want to be a direct, active participant in the creation, facilitation, and augmentation of the joy and happiness of others.

It is vague enough to allow for great flexibility in the approach, yet steadfast in its purpose. This is the end to which I intend to dedicate myself for now. May it guide me well, if only to the next more appropriate star around which I orient my life.

All my lovin',

- Blake.

Day 25

Pride

1. I'm proud that the woman at the bar said, "You bring so much happiness here! You have such a great vibe!"
2. I'm proud that I took time to stop and smell the roses on the Camino today by doing Tai Chi along the way.
3. I'm proud that I'm stopping to journal and do pride and gratitude before visiting the city today, because they are both so helpful for me.

Gratitude

1. I'm grateful for the hilarious video message Jennifer sent me today. It was excellent to have her with me on the Camino.
2. I'm grateful for the splendid conditions and weather on what was perhaps the last quiet day of my Camino.
3. I'm grateful for the laughs and good vibes I shared with Olivia on our walk today.

Day 26

LUGO → SAN ROMAN

18 km / 11.19 mi.

*N*ursing a hangover after a lovely party last night which included lots of wine, tapas, a delicious meal, and more party, beer and merriment than necessary.

We all slept wonderfully in our little albergue, with the sheets, and blankets, and silence.

We were the only 5 people in our 14 person dorm (apart from 1 random pilgrim who stole Kyle's bed while we were away) so there was no one to rustle bags, or turn on lights, or disturb us.

We slept until 10:00, then had a very slow morning drinking coffee and eating on the terrace before setting off at the early hour of 12:30.

The walk was short and uneventful, but pleasant. We walked 18 KM (11.19 mi.) and, apart from heavy rain for the last 20 minutes, there was little of note.

Tonight has been a very pleasant evening of my little seven person Camino Family (Kyle: Kiwi, Luke: Irish, Gabriel: Colombian, Jacob: Canadian, Abigail: Danish, Olivia: Ukranian) sitting by the wood burning stove in our cold albergue, all squeezed onto two tiny couches.

We drank wine, and chatted, and laughed, and ate chocolate, and got warm from the fire and the body heat of the people pressed against us.

Santiago is only three days away, and I honestly don't want to arrive. Life on the Camino is truly a delight. I will miss it dearly, and don't wish for it to end.

All my lovin',

- Blake.

Day 26

Pride

1. I'm proud I'm learning to choose when to express what I feel and think.
2. I'm proud of my photos that I've taken on this trip.
3. I'm proud of the friend I've made in el Camino.

Gratitude

1. I'm grateful for the cozy evening by the fire with my tiny Camino Family.
2. I'm grateful for my friends, and all their support in my Camino.
3. I'm grateful for the simplicity of Camino Life.

Day 27

SAN ROMAN → MELIDE

28 km / 17.39 mi

oday we said farewell to the Primitivo, and what a farewell it was. The Sun was shining, the scenery was green and quiet, and the medieval towns we passed through were still and peaceful, a heaviness of time pressing down upon their winding, narrow streets. We passed hardly a single pilgrim, and had the Camino all to ourselves.

The morning air was frosty and full of mist gleaming with yellow morning Sun. As the old gravel road, built by the Romans and lined with towering eucalyptus and withered oaks, descended into a valley, I was met with a wall of fog, sitting neatly and completely, and geometrically on top of the entire valley 100 meters (109.36 yd.) ahead and 100 meters (109.36 yd.) below.

It was as though a glass box had been placed over the valley and filled with the blue-white smoke of a million cigarettes, it's borders and limits clear-cut and final. The pilgrims walking before me were dwarfed by the massive cloud formation until they suddenly disappeared into it.

Olivia, Abigail, and I walked the whole way together, the miles passing quickly under our feet, as easily and carelessly as the conversation and laughter flowed between us. I couldn't have hoped for a nicer day, which was made all the more special by the likelihood of it being the

last quiet day on the Camino. We've two days to Santiago and as of tomorrow we'll be walking on the Camino Frances, the busiest of all the Caminos. I've been warned to expect quite a shock, as we go from seeing 50 pilgrims a day to hundreds.

Though today was about as good a day on the Camino as anyone could ask for, the time after arrival to Melide has been unexpectedly tumultuous in that space between my ears. After my shower, I walked to a cafe with Jacob for a drink and a bite to eat. Suddenly stricken with extreme tiredness, I found myself warding off a wave of anxiety catalyzed, as it often is, by a seemingly innocuous event.

Thinking I had ordered only a tiny serving of tortilla, I was given a full order, which cost as much as €7.00, on top of the beers I had bought

Jacob and myself. My brain spun.

"Money. Mistake. Not what I wanted."

"How did you misorder this?"

"Money."

"Not hungry. Can't save. Money. Idiot."

Then the mood was set. Luckily Olivia and Jacob enjoyed some, so none was wasted.

Though it was unpleasant, I was glad to see my initial reaction was to fight the anxiety, rather than simply crumble under its grip. I wasn't immediately victorious, and in fact it took nearly two-and-a-half hours for the feeling to pass, but every time it started gaining ground, or made another push to take over my thoughts, I stood firm and thought, "No. this is just the anxiety. It isn't real. Fight it. Breathe. Edit your photos. Write in your journal. Do your Pride and Gratitude. This will pass."

And I'm happy to report that it already has. I'm glad to see that my reaction time is better and faster, and that I'm learning to understand the connection between my mind and body; between physical weariness and mental fortitude; between anxiety and reality.

Today, unexpectedly, Olivia told me, "I think you need to work on your apologizing."

I was taken a bit aback, but curious. "Oh?"

"Yes," she answered, "You're horrible at this."

I didn't even try to fight. I wanted to hear what she had to say, and to learn. "Okay. Thanks for telling me that. What can I do better?"

"You said you were apologizing to make yourself feel better. This is terrible."

She was right. I had said that. Of course, I was, in my discomfort, being sarcastic. I believe my exact words were, "In order to make myself feel better," with a wry smirk, "I got you a very tiny gift." Her rejection was swift and steadfast.

Now I can see why. She thought I was serious.

"Well," I said, "I'm glad you told me that. But I didn't mean that. I was being sarcastic."

"Oh! Really!?"

"Yes. I mean, only a crazy person would say that and mean it. I'm sorry though. It wasn't at all the right time to be sarcastic."

"Well I didn't know that. I thought you were serious!"

Our conversation was cut short before we could bring it to a clean close by Abigail's arrival at the cafe we had entered. Still, after a few moments of awkwardness, the rest of the afternoon was spent pleasantly.

I'm tempted to bring it up, if only to give her the apology I feel she deserves, but then, sometimes it's best to let sleeping dogs lie, so I'm a bit unsure if I should.

Perhaps I'll just thank her for being honest and open about an uncomfortable subject, which is a quality I certainly appreciate in a friend.

Tonight we're eating pulpo (octopus), which is a specialty in this city. I'm looking forward to a nice meal with my lovely Camino Family, who has been joined today by Abigail's parents, who are finishing up the Camino Frances this year, which they've been walking over the years all the way from Denmark.

All my lovin',

- Blake.

Pride

1. I'm proud that 30 KM (18.64 mi.) with no real food in my stomach was a piece of cake! I'm in great shape!

2. I'm proud that I've been staying on top of my psyche this afternoon. I'm tired, and my anxiety is trying to get the better of me.

3. I'm proud that I was so open to criticism today and didn't fight, but listened.

Gratitude

1. I'm grateful for our clean, lovely albergue.

2. I'm grateful for Olivia telling me I'm horrible at apologizing. Feedback from friends is important.

3. I'm grateful for the wonderful final day of the Primitivo.

Day 28

MELIDE → O PEDROUZO

33 KM / 20.51 mi.

Today we got another fairly late start, leaving the cafe, two coffees in our bellies, at 9:30 to begin today's stage of the Camino. It was the first day walking along the Camino Frances, and although the difference in the quantity and type of pilgrims was glaring, if unpleasant, it wasn't nearly as bad as I had anticipated, probably thanks to our distance from the end of the peak season.

I must admit I found it quite difficult to reserve my judgement for those pilgrims who, based on the freshness of their attire, have come only to walk the final 100 KM (62.14 mi.) of the Camino Frances, the official cut-off for those who wish to receive a Compostela. It was even more difficult to reserve judgement for the people walking with only day bags, who are using luggage transport services to carry their rolly-suitcases from hotel to hotel, while they walk with only what they need for the day. Still, to each his own Camino. I suppose we all have different things we want to get out of the Camino, and different reasons for coming here, so it makes sense that we all have different ways of completing our Caminos, and I shouldn't feel better than anyone. That would be, in fact, very contrary to the pilgrim's spirit.

I spent about half the day walking and chatting with Olivia, and the other half walking alone. It was a very long day, but very pleasant. In spite of the business, I still found myself all alone for about 90 minutes of the walk today, which was really enjoyable, especially since it was the last day of the Camino. Tomorrow we'll be in Santiago by noon. I really can't believe it's been a month. The time has simply flown by.

Today I felt a small rush of anxiety at the thought of returning home, and I was glad for the reminder that I am not perfect. It was good to have a moment to remind myself that I will almost certainly have a few panicky moments when I get back to Berlin, and from where I was standing today, I was able to remind myself that such panic is normal, and that it is in no way a reflection of my progress.

I am very likely to, in the moment of that anxiety, give in to the whirlwind of my thoughts, which will probably include me thinking that I've made no progress, that I'm as broken as I always felt, and all hope is lost.

But from where I'm standing today, I would remind myself that such a moment does not negate my progress, or how far I've come. It does not mean all is lost. It just means that I'm overwhelmed in that moment, but it will pass, faster than it used to, because I am better and know how to cope, and control my thoughts.

I even started thinking about who I'll call when that moment strikes, and who I'll turn to for help, and I was gladdened by the thought that, thanks to the Camino, I have even more people to turn to for comfort, support, and understanding.

I'm not ready for the Camino to end, so I'm very glad that I'll have three days to carry on to Finesterre. And while I'm not ready to arrive in Santiago, I am looking forward to celebrating the completing of a very big, beautiful goal, so pregnant with meaning, for which I had to work so hard, with so many people who feel exactly the same.

My words are failing me tonight, and I feel like I'm not really expressing myself well, but I suppose it is enough to say that I am happy, and calm, and feel an overwhelming sense of how fortunate I am to have been able to walk the Camino. It has truly been a wonder.

All my lovin',

- Blake.

P.S. Abigail's father, who is a physiotherapist, had a look at my knee and assured me that it is neither serious nor permanent. I just need to be careful and treat it well until it is all healed. That was really a relief.

Pride

1. I'm proud that Olivia, and many others, see me as a very positive person. What a change!
2. I'm proud that I'm already making a support plan for when I get home.
3. I'm proud that I'm excited about the future, rather than afraid of it.

Gratitude

1. I'm grateful that I found some time completely alone on the Camino today.
2. I'm grateful for the lack of rain we've had on the Camino.
3. I'm grateful for my excellent physical health.

Day 29

O PEDROUZO → SANTIAGO DE COMPOSTELA

20 KM / 12.43 mi.

I DID IT!!!! I completed the Camino de Santiago!!! I am overjoyed and overwhelmed by how lucky I feel to have had the good health, and the time, and the money, and the headspace to walk the Camino, and walk it well and in a way that I can truly enjoy and appreciate it. It has been a pleasure and a privilege, and I cannot begin to express my gratitude for this opportunity, and all that I have learned, and lived, and experienced.

On day 20, from Bodenaya to Campiello, which was then and remains my favorite day of the Camino, Anthony, a 68 year-old Dutch man on his 7th Camino, asked me what I thought of the Camino.

"I don't really know if I can describe it," I said.

"So don't," he replied with a smile.

And I won't. Suffice it to say that there are two words that come to mind when I think about how to sum up this experience.

Significant.

Consequential.

Two words, cold, calculated, far too unevocative to be considered fitting for what is meant to be a life-changing, spiritual experience. Yet, they are as accurate as they are stoic, and I am so pleased that for me they ring true; that this was a significant, consequential experience.

And yet it must be said that the massive anticlimax of arrival to Santiago may well be the Camino's most important lesson. Today was one of the days on the Camino I least enjoyed. The way was full of pilgrims of all sorts, the scenery wasn't especially beautiful, the weather was a mix of fog, cloud, drizzle, and rain, the sky seemingly just above our heads, and steeped in a grey so deep as to suck the color right out of the world around it.

An hour away from the Cathedral, the rain truly began to fall, not heavy enough to impede the journey, or force us to take cover, but heavy enough to require ponchos, and to soak our feet.

I had initially readied myself for the anticlimax and reminded myself throughout the trip that I would likely feel nothing in Santiago, but I suppose I had sort of imagined it would at least be a sunny day, or that I would be at a minimum in good spirits. I had also prepared myself for the hoards of pilgrims milling about the plaza, and the heaviness of a journey come to an end. I figured I would be happy to arrive in Santiago in any form. There was one scenario, however, I had truly not prepared myself for; one scenario I dared not even imagine or dream about for fear of jinxing the final stage of my journey: arriving at the plaza under the heavy, plastic cover of a dripping wet rain poncho. And as we approached closer and closer, step by step, feet ever wetter and clouds ever heavier, it became clear that this one scenario about which I dared not speak, was slowly becoming the cold hard reality waiting to greet me with dripping arms at the end of this journey; my journey.

I looked to Olivia, also looking ridiculous, wrapped under the skin tight neon orange hood of her jacket and sheathed in a fluorescent turquoise rain poncho, converting her slender, feminine frame into an amorphous blob.

She was smiling. And I was glad. She looked to me and reminded me that this is exactly the finale we should hope for: So anticlimactic as to be hilarious; so undesirable as to serve as a reminder to us, to anyone who ever asks the obligatory question: "What was it like to arrive in Santiago?"

"Very unpleasant," the only answer I can think of, will forever hammer home that tired cliché, " The journey is the destination." And never has that ever felt truer for me than today, as we inched closer to the official end of our pilgrimages.

I resigned myself to the fate of my long-awaited, much anticipated journey, and was so thankful to have Olivia with me to remind me of this lesson, and to suffer this unfortunate fate with me.

Only moments away from the cathedral, the rain stopped. Olivia and I threw off our rain ponchos, shoved them in our bags, and made a Bee line for the plaza, where so many pilgrims would be in the midst of their own finales.

And while it was anticlimactic, it was very beautiful all the same. We were happy and felt good to be there. Abigail and her parents arrived minutes later, and we all hugged and took photos before heading off to see the remains of St. James the Greater, one of the twelve Apostles, for whom all the Caminos have been created.

I donated the €5.00 the woman in Grado had entrusted me with, and thanked him for imparting this experience which defies description upon me.

After an excellent peregrino menu, one of the best I had, and checking into the hotel, we went back to the city, where we drank a beer and came across pilgrim after pilgrim we had met along the way.

I had debated whether or not I wanted to attend the pilgrim's mass held in the Cathedral. Between my turbulent history with the Catholic church, my agnosticism, and my penchant for blasphemy, I wasn't sure it was the best idea, or the most appropriate. Finally, I decided it would be a nice experience, and thought the pomp, circumstance, and ceremony might be a nice finish to the day; might inflate the meaning of an otherwise fairly flat finish.

Olivia and I sat in the very last row in the ancient wooden pew looking directly upon the gawdy, ornate altar. As the organs blasted and a priest sang, I cried. From where I was seated I could see a priest waiting patiently in a confessional, reading, passing the time for the confessions that he wouldn't be receiving. I haven't been to confession since I was a child. I always disliked it, and to this day think it is a disgraceful thing to make a child do, but when I saw him, I knew I would confess.

I, having not been to confession for more than 6 months (not to mention having denounced God, Jesus, the Holy Spirit, and the entire establishment of the Catholic Church) am not technically allowed to receive the Eucharist. But I wanted to. It called to me.

Before leaving for the Camino, Alon and I were speaking about the Camino, and he said something that struck me.

"Symbols have meaning and power if we give them meaning."

And there is little more symbolic than the Eucharist.

I wanted this moment, this punctuation mark, this turning point, this moment of purging, of being cleansed, of starting over. I needed it. And I had walked 500 miles for it. And as I received the Eucharist, I cried. As it dissolved, the tears formed and fell. And when Mass ended, I went straight to the priest in the confessional.

He almost looked surprised when I asked him if he was receiving confession.

"Of course," he responded in Spanish, with a smile.

I walked around to the side and kneeled.

"What would you like to confess?" he asked with warmth.

The sobbing began. "I've committed the sin of not loving myself, and of considering killing myself many, many times."

"You're confessing this because you're good," he responded. "Don't worry. Where have you come from?"

"Irún."

"And how far is that?"

"850 kilometers."

"My God! That's far!"

"Yes, it is. And I've come to do the Camino to start over, to start a new life for myself."

He was kind, and warm, and comforting; a far cry from what I remembered confession being like. He asked me about where I was from, and my family, and my life in Berlin. He reiterated that not many people come to confess after the Camino, and that the fact that I had come to confess was a sign of the person I am, and the good upbringing I'd had. He told me a story about Pope John Paul II, and how nervous he was when named Pope. This is what he was reading about, which he had told me he was recounting so I could, "relax, calm down, and cry in peace."

"He said the Holy Spirit calmed his soul. This is something only the holy spirit can do. And it will calm yours as well."

In the middle of the prayer, he stopped, and laughed. "I'm sorry, I forgot the prayer due to being so emotional!" He started again, and finished, and absolved me of my sins, and asked me to say one Hail Mary as a penetance, probably such a small fine as walking 500 miles made up the rest of my penetance. I think this was a very emotional confession for him as well. He asked if he could hug me, and I was glad for the reassuring embrace. He repeated that I was good, and that I should dedicate myself to taking care of my family in both the U.S., and in Berlin, and assured me that all was well, and I was well.

I went to the pew and struggled to say a Hail Mary. I looked up the prayer on Google and prayed. After making the sign of the cross, I looked up at the altar, and a thought came into my mind:

"Y así, se cambió una vida entera."

"And like that, an entire life changed."

Olivia was also in a pew crying. We sat beside one another and cried, then we hugged, warmly, full of love and comfort.

I didn't confess because I wanted forgiveness from a God I don't believe in. I confessed because Alon is right. Symbols have meaning and power. And this was my symbol. I wasn't speaking to a priest, or to God. I was speaking to myself, to the universe. I was admitting openly that I have wronged myself, and in doing so, making a vow, outloud, into a void, an energy, a world of spirituality, that a transformation has taken place; that I won't continue a life of cruelty to myself; that I will love myself, and in doing so, as the priest suggested, better serve the universe in which I live, of which I am a part as beautiful, unique, and valuable as anything else within it.

"Y así, se cambió una vida entera."

As I left the cathedral, the words of the priest's sermon rang in my ears:

"We must be sowers of peace and happiness in the lives of those around us."

How fitting.

What a reminder of the mission I have set for myself. It felt as though the universe was tipping its hat in my direction.

Gavin, the hospitalero from Bodenaya, said, "El verdadero Camino empieza después de Santiago." "The True Camino begins after Santiago."

I am excited for it. I am ready for it. And I only had to walk 850 KM (528.17 mi.) to feel that I am.

All my lovin',

- Blake.

<u>Addendum:</u> September 19th, 2017 - While walking today, it occurred to me that this confession was indeed a moment of absolution, but not from a higher power. It was a moment of absolution from myself. It was a moment in which I not only declared to the universe that I recognize the error of the way I've been living my life, living with myself, and renounce the mistakes of my past, but also forgave myself for a lifetime of transgressions against myself. I took that moment to wipe the slate clean, to start afresh, to begin this next phase of my Camino from a place of purity and self-love; from a place in which I have nothing to hold against myself; from a place in which there is no past to regret, and only the rest of a lifetime to look forward to. Tears have seldom felt so cathartic.

Day 29

Pride

1. I am proud I walked all 815 KM (506.42 mi.) to Santiago de Compostela!
2. I am proud that so many people know my name, and were happy to greet and congratulate me.
3. I'm proud that I, once again, finished what I started.

Gratitude

1. I'm grateful that I was healthy enough to make it to Santiago.
2. I am grateful that I have had the amazing good fortune to walk the Camino.
3. I'm grateful that Olivia has been with me and kept me sane and clear about the silliness of it all.

Day 30

SANTIAGO DE COMPOSTELA → VILASERIO

33 KM / 20.51 mi.

*L*ast night we had drinks to celebrate until about 2:00, and got to bed at 2:30. Olivia and I awoke at 7:00 in order to get to the pilgrim's office, get in line to get our compostellas before the doors opened at 8:00, then head out once again to start our trip to Finnisterre, the end of the world.

I spent the morning walking with Olivia. At one point I stopped for coffee and Olivia kept going. About two hours later I came to a place where I could see the next large village about three KM (1.86 mi.) off in the distance.

"Lovely," I thought, "Olivia's probably there having a coffee, and I'll probably walk right past her. Oh, and I bet Abigail will be there with…" I stopped. I knew Abigail was still in Santiago with her parents and wouldn't leave for Finnisterre until tomorrow, but at this point, she's become a fixture of my Camino. We spent 23 of 29 days walking together, and 22 nights in the same albergue, and since we met only 2 days were spent hiking apart, and 3 nights in a different albergue!

I was saddened by the realization that we will hike no more together, and although I'll probably see her in Fenisterre, our Camino together has come to an end.

The Camino was very quiet today, in spite of the number of pilgrims on it. Everyone I passed gave off a somber air; the air of people in airport terminals and hotel lobbies who are waiting to board the flights taking them home, or check out of the rooms that were their vacation retreats. Although there are three days to Finisterre, Summer Camp has definitely ended, and that fact seemed to hang heavy in the air today.

Still, it was a beautiful walk, and I was totally alone for a fair portion of it, and with Olivia for the rest. After 33 KM (20.51 mi.), we wound up at a beautiful albergue with a massive garden with sunset views overlooking endless hilly countryside, and a huge fireplace, inside of which Olivia and I sat chatting and writing all evening.

I'm so glad to have three more days on my Camino, and I hope they'll be as beautiful as today. I'm trying to take them very easy, and even drank a beer on one of the latter legs of today's walk.

All my lovin',

– Blake.

Day 30

Pride

1. I am proud that I walked 33 KM on 4.5 hours of sleep.
2. I am proud that I so effortlessly decided to change albergues and not worry about it.
3. I am proud that so many people care about me and my life.

Gratitude

1. I am grateful for the wonderful albergue here at Villa Casa.
2. I am grateful for the Sunny weather we had all afternoon, which was so nice after so many days of clouds and fog.
3. I am grateful for the company I've had on the Camino.

Day 31

VILASERIO → HOSPITAL

25 KM / 15.53 mi.

Wednesday, September 20th, 2017

no time recorded

*A*nother lovely day on the camino, but one with little to report back about.

The morning was slow, as Olivia and I sipped mediocre cups of filter coffee in the warmth of that wonderful, cozy albergue. I sat on the porch and watched the pink sky retreat behind the hills as it gave way to blue, and a thick white mist glide across the valleys.

The Sun shone the entire day and the walk itself was relaxing and easy, winding through tiny villages, and curling up over and around graceful hills. We walked very slowly, needing nearly seven hours to cover the measly 25 KM (15.53 mi.).

My emotions are turbulent, switching quickly from one to the next; from happiness at being on the Camino during such beautiful weather to sadness that it's all ending, back to happiness, and all around the spectrum of emotions.

Still, I've finished today in a very good mood and am happy about it all, even if it's all ending.

As it all comes to a close, and my Camino days are numbered, I have a

really hard time imagining myself spending nine days doing normal tourism in Portugal. I just can't picture it. So much so that I'm now considering skipping my nine days of normal tourism in Portugal, where I thought of spending a couple days in a few different cities, and taking a bus to Porto, and walking 10 more days to Santiago on the Camino Portugues.

All my lovin',

- Blake.

Pride

1. I am proud that I always pay my debts, and always pay my round.

2. I am proud that 25 KM is now considered a very easy day of walking.

3. I am proud that I have learned so much on the Camino, and have been open enough to learn at all.

Gratitude

1. I am grateful for the gorgeous, cool, sunny weather we had today, and on so many days of the Camino.

2. I am grateful for the excellent morning I had at Casa Villa.

3. I am grateful for El Camino and the opportunity to walk it today.

Day 32

HOSPITAL → MUXÍA

27 km / 16.77 mi.

Thursday, September 21st, 2017

no time recorded

As we sat in the albergue owner's cafe at 8:00 sipping our coffee, we watched the pouring rain with apprehension. Passing pilgrims, wet to the bone in spite of their flailing rain ponchos slowly filled the cafe, marching slowly toward refuge one by one.

I was dreading walking in this rain. I never liked being wet, or wearing wet clothes, and I like being cold even less, so the prospect of spending a day walking with soggy feet and wet clothing didn't exactly speak to me.

I almost began feeling grumpy as I got up to start putting on my rain poncho, and thought, "I really don't want to walk in the rain." Then, suddenly, I realized, no one was forcing me to. I could walk when I felt like it, and if I didn't want to walk in the rain, if I would be happier to wait for it to lighten or stop, then I could do exactly that. So I got another coffee, and waited, glad for yet another sign of the personal development I find myself undergoing.

Waiting was the right choice. The rain only intensified gradually until about 9:30, when it stopped altogether, and Olivia and I headed out.

The walk was quiet and peaceful, and terribly emotional. Somehow it

felt heavy, pregnant with memories, meaning, symbolism, energy, and nostalgia. Olivia and I barely spoke most of the way, but I was comforted by her presence, always within earshot in one direction or the other.

About halfway I found myself awash in a very strong desire to be with my family. But not just to be with my family. I wanted to be with them in our home. I wanted to be home.

I mentioned this to Olivia, and she replied, "That's funny. I never felt homesick."

Homesick. That word hung in the air. I hadn't used the word myself, and hadn't thought it, either. But based on my description of my feelings, Olivia named the emotion. Homesick.

I was struck by the thought of being homesick. I've never, ever, in all my life been homesick. Until that moment. There was a comfort in the notion of being with my family, in our cozy little home.

It rained a bit again for about an hour, only after, of course, I had taunted the grey clouds, silently hanging above us for two hours, by finally removing my rain poncho.

When the rain subsided, in the distance, a blue hole opened in the clouds. I was filled with hope that it would widen and eventually swallow up all the grey.

With about one-and-a-half hours left in our walk, we saw the sea for the first time since we left the Camino del Norte. At the first whiff of ocean air blowing into my nostrils on a strong sea breeze I burst into tears. I had missed the ocean. So I went to find it again. And I found it.

We continued, silently, walking to Muxía, and were finally, after a long descent, at sea level, and greeted with a small, silent beach full of large, marbley rocks, polished smooth by the ocean. The Atlantic Ocean.

Olivia, about 50 meters (54.68 yd..) ahead, was standing in the surf. I followed suit. In my head, Finnisterre was the end, so, for a moment, the gravity of our arrival to the ocean was lost on me. And when I touched the icy water, I thought, "Wow. I've never seen the Atlantic Ocean. The Atlantic Ocean. I'm at the Ocean. I made it to the Ocean." And then I wept with joy and sadness and every emotion I'm capable of feeling. I had crossed Spain, from one side to the other, and made it all the way to the Ocean with only my two feet and my will power to carry me. And I never thought I was capable of such a thing.

I've never felt prouder.

Olivia and I walked into the quiet, tiny town and checked into our albergue. We went to the hill overlooking the city, where the Ocean slams powerfully against the rocks of the peninsula. Picturesque doesn't begin to describe it. The Sun, which had come out to greet us as soon as we arrived in Muxía, cast a warm glow over everything and the natural beauty of the waves, bursting into the air in streams as they slammed the rocks was contrasted by the architectural beauty of a stone cathedral, delicate domes atop massive towers made entirely of rocks which seemed themselves to emanate the Sun's light, staring out to sea like a mariner's widow, itself accompanied by a lone, rusty, white lighthouse.

Putting the beauty of the scene I witnessed into words is a futile effort, as it was a beauty made powerful by the emotional baggage I had carried with me to get there. But it was so beautiful that Jacob, upon seeing it, began weeping uncontrollably, and couldn't stop, he told us. A 71 year-old playboy who has lived a life most could never dream of, wept at the sight.

After dinner we returned and watched the sunset, Kyle, Olivia, and I, along with Naomi, a Slovakian girl we'd seen in some of our albergues. It was magnificent, and the way the clouds formed tiny rows of cotton balls, rows which repeated into the infinity beyond the horizon as the Sun set behind them, I can see why people thought this was the end of the world.

I realized today that I am considering continuing on the Portuguese Camino because I'm scared to leave the Camino. Fear is motivating me to continue walking, as it has for so many years. I'm not sure that's the best reason to walk. So I have another day or two to think it over.

Abigail will be meeting us in Finisterre tomorrow, after we walk the last and final stage of our Camino. Jacob and Olivia and I will walk together. I haven't walked with Jacob on the Camino since we arrived in La Vega, so I'm pleased for the chance to walk one more time with him.

Tomorrow we walk to the end of the world.

All my lovin',

- Blake.

Pride

1. I am proud that I walked with my own two feet, <u>literally</u> all the way across Spain.
2. I am proud that I am in touch with my emotions, but not controlled by them.
3. I am proud that I have journaled <u>every single</u> day of the Camino, and will always have this document of my journey.

Gratitude

1. I am grateful that the rain stopped this morning before we walked, and the Sun came out this afternoon when we arrived in Muxía.
2. I am grateful that I have walked the entire Camino in good health and unharmed the whole way.
3. I am grateful Kyle, Abigail, Jacob, and I are in the same albergue, and will walk the Camino together, one last time.

Day 33

MUXÍA → FINISTERRE

27 KM / 16.77 mi.

Friday, September 22nd, 2017

no time recorded

oday, on our last day of the Camino, to quote Jacob directly, "We were not fuckin' around!" We walked the hilly 27 KM (16.78 mi.) through forests and along the coast, the faint sound of crashing waves and eucalyptus leaves rattling in the breeze ever present, in four-and-a-half hours, leaving at 8:30, and arriving, after a 30 minute coffee break, at 13:30.

We walked so quickly, and so easily, that I didn't believe the city I saw at 2 KM off (1.24 mi.), squeezed right against the sea, was our destination until I saw a sign reading Fistera. It's incredible the kind of shape the Camino has whipped me into. My back no longer aches under the (admittedly small) weight of my bag. My feet don't hurt. My muscles aren't sore. I felt I could have walked another 10 KM (6.21 mi.) without batting an eye.

Of course, the fantastic weather, sunny and cool and full of ocean breezes, as well as the pleasant company made for smooth sailing. Additionally, the emotional weight of the last few days had drained out of me on the beach in Muxía. Today didn't feel at all like "the last day." It felt like a bonus day, just something I was lucky to have. That, combined with my excitement about seeing Abigail, kept my feet light and fast.

I spent the first hour walking with Jacob and chatting lightheartedly, mostly listening to his always humorous stories, as we had done for literally hundreds of miles together.

There were quite a few pilgrims moving in both directions between Fisterra and Muxía, necessitating far more "Buen Caminos" than normal; than desirable for a quiet morning walk.

But, by the time we arrived at a bar at the halfway point, I had passed pretty much all the pilgrims going to Fisterra, and all the pilgrims going to Muxía had made it beyond the halfway point. Olivia was incredibly quiet while we drank coffee, so I walked ahead of her, and although she was never more than 100 meters (109.36 yd.) behind me, we didn't exchange a word for the last 15 KM (9.32 mi.) of the walk. I could tell she wanted to be alone, and I did as well.

It was very fortunate that I crossed only 3 pilgrims on the rest of the way meaning I was totally alone for my last bit of Camino.

Admittedly, it wasn't all fun. I spent the first hour after my break angrily cursing my bad luck, as I had, over the last two days, found myself COMPLETELY COVERED in bed bug bites, from shoulders to toes. Once again, no one I know has a single one, and I'm covered. While I'm glad no one else is struggling with the itchiness of it, and the penetrating thoughts of helplessness and violation the night predators have sowed in my sleepless nights, I must confess that the injustice of my solitary suffering, not to mention the sheer mystery of how I was the sole victim in every albergue in which we all stayed, at this point a mystery far greater than the origin of life, or what lies beyond the grave, had worked me into a state of aggressive frustration, made all the more intense by the constant reminder of my torment with every itch, and every oozing bite.

So, I spent an hour getting angry, calming down, getting worked up, reminding myself to look at the trees, angry, let it go, furious, chilled.

It was a dizzying dance, but one I was glad to see I was dancing. Normally, I'd just succumb to the anger for hours. So, while I had to keep up the back and forth longer than I would have liked, it's beautiful to know that I'm learning the moves; learning to be mindful, and present, and in control of my emotions.

The last hour was a delight; alone, quiet, content, excited, just me and the Camino, all the way to a very early finish in Fistera

As the edge of the woods crept closer, bringing with it the official close, in my mind, of the Camino, I spoke aloud, with tears in my eyes, and thanked the Camino.

> For the incredible weather
> for the breathtaking scenery
> for the lessons it taught me
> for the people it brought me
> for the ups and the downs
> for the confidence it instilled in me.
> for the excitement, and health, and positivity
> for the tiny villages,
> for the time alone, which I truly needed
> for the beaches and oceans
> for every single tiny little arrow
> for keeping me safe and uninjured, and able to continue

for guiding me constantly, so I could be free to enjoy and think
for the lessons it will continue to bestow upon me.
for everything. Genuinely, for everything.

I laughed. "Well," I said with a teary smile, "you can keep the fucking bed bugs. But thanks for everything else."

Moments later I was out of the woods, and was called by Jacob, who was sat at the first bar in Finisterre, having a beer.

Olivia arrived moments later, and we all drank a toast.

"To the End of the World."

We were all three amazed at how quickly and easily we walked today, and were all somehow glad, and I think, a little sad.

After checking into our lovely albergue, clinical, yet cozy, and perfectly suited to the needs of a pilgrim, and showering, and giving everything in my bag to the laundry service in the hopes of drowning and overheating any bed bugs creeping in the seams of my clothes and sleeping bag, Olivia and I went to the port for a drink and to write in our journals, a habit we had developed, and which I really enjoy. Sitting together, writing about our unique interpretations of our shared experiences.

I had rehearsed the speech I wanted to make to her a few times on the Camino today.

"Olivia, I'm going to get soppy and emotional for just a minute, if you'll let me. I really need to express my feelings, and I don't know if we'll get another chance today." She smiled, maybe a little apprehensively, and nodded. "I just want to say what a pleasure its been to share my Camino with you. I've really learned a lot, I think, from you, and your perspective on life, and had a lot of laughs thanks to you. You made my camino much more interesting, and much more fun. Of course, I'm imperfect, and even in the short time we've known each other, I've made some mistakes. I can't fix them, I can't change them, but I can say that I am genuinely sorry for them. And I want to say how much it means to me that you continued to share your Camino with me, even after I made them. You didn't have to. You could have said, 'Fuck that guy,' and walked on, but you didn't. You chose, I think, to forgive me, and continue to share your Camino with me, and for that I am truly grateful. So, as a token of my friendship, and more importantly, as a token of my appreciation for your friendship, I want to give you a small, tiny thing, if you will accept it, to remember me by. You can throw it away or give it back, but I'd like you to have it."

And I gave her a tiny pin which I'd been carrying on my backpack, which she told me she was jealous of. A little pin of a friendly, yellow arrow.

She took it and smiled. "So," I continued, "maybe you can put it somewhere where you'll see it frequently, and it can remind you that you're always on the right Camino. You just need to follow the little arrows."

She was very thankful, and I was so grateful to have given her the apology she deserved, and that she accepted it. We hugged tightly and warmly.

She peered at me with her striking green eyes, made all the more intense by her thick, swooping black eyeliner, and struggled to say something, then paused. "I'm not good in…"

I cut her off. "You don't need to say anything. Really. We've walked together for hundreds of miles. I already know how you feel...I think."

She nodded and smiled. "Thank you. Thank you."

We drank our beer, and walked to the Municipal albergue, where we got our Fisterano, the certificate certifying that we had completed the pilgrimage to Fisterra. We met Jacob there, and the three of us went to the grocery store to buy supplies for the picnic dinner we would have at the lighthouse, where the 0 KM mark is located, 3 KM (1.86 mi.) from the city center.

Abigail and her parents arrived just when we came back from the grocery store. Kyle couldn't walk, suddenly suffering from tendonitis, so Abigail came in his place. We had sandwiches, chips, olives, chocolate, and 4 bottles of delicious Spanish red wine.

So, Jacob, Olivia, Abigail, and I, with Gabriel, who had been in Fisterra for a day already, walked the 3 KM (1.86 mi.) to the lighthouse. After the obligatory photos with the 0 KM mark, we sat on the rocks and ate and drank as we watched a magnificent sunset unfold before us. Just as the sun reached the horizon, a massive boat, sailing exactly on the line where the water meets the sky miles away, began to sail between us and the disappearing Sun. we were in awe of the hilarity and improbability of it all. The setting Sun was covered by the massive ship, only a shadow in the distance, and when the ship sailed past, the Sun was already gone. We would have been annoyed for the interruption if not for the amusement it caused in us.

We left after the wine was gone, and the sky was dark. I don't think I appreciated how special it was to have Jacob, Abigail, and Olivia there for that final punctuation mark on our trip, because I don't think it occurred to me that it was the punctuation mark. I was so lucky to have shared my Camino with them, and insanely fortunate to be able to share such a beautiful moment, all together, still together, as we brought our journey to a close together.

As the Sun was setting, Jacob said, "well, it was sure a pleasure to walk so much with all of you. You all made me feel very welcome, so thank you."

We all thanked him for his company, stories, and most of all, inspiration.

He continued, "And, I think Blake was the glue that held us all together. So, here's to Blake." He raised his plastic cup full of wine, and the others mimicked him.

"To Blake," they all said with smiles.

And I'm so grateful to have been the glue, if that is indeed what I was. I'm so lucky to have been able to bring such nice, interesting people into my life, and to bring them into each other's.

Walking back, on the dark road under a billion stars, Abigail scooped up a tiny baby goat, walking alone down the road, probably looking for its herd, and almost certain to be hit by a car. She carried it like a newborn all the way down the road, as we laughed.

She tried putting him down in a safe place, and we ran away, but it followed screaming, "Sarah! Sarah! Sarah!" to which Abigail replied, "No, goat, it's Abigail!"

Eventually a car stopped, having nearly hit the goat, and lamented the owner, who leaves his goats to wander freely in the hills around the lighthouse. She called the owner, who came two minutes later in his car to pick it up. Abigail was so proud we had saved the goat, and I was glad to have one more memory to punctuate today which was, indeed, a tremendous occasion made commonplace by the habitual nature the rhythm of the Camino had condemned it to. I think we all forgot that it was a tremendous occasion, because I don't think we realized that tomorrow we wouldn't simply rise and walk; that tomorrow our Caminos would finally split, separating us until, if, they cross again. It's just as well. If it hadn't felt so ordinary, like just another lovely evening on the Camino, I'd have spent the whole night crying.

After many beers, and much laughter at the tales of Jacob's MANY sexual escapades, sat in a bar called, "The World Family," full of Germans with flowing clothes and dreadlocks, we went back to the individual sleeping pods in our albergue.

Watching Jacob and Olivia say goodbye made me sad. I told him and Abigail to wake me before they left.

I'll save my goodbyes for tomorrow.

I'm staying an extra day here to gather my thoughts, and figure out my next plan. I'm going to Portugal, but I don't know what I'll do there: walk the Camino Portugues or visit some cities as a tourist. I guess I'll think about it tomorrow, probably with lots of tears in my eyes.

All my lovin',

- Blake.

Day 33

Pride

1. I'm proud I walked to the end of the Earth.
2. I'm proud that Jacob said I was the glue that kept this Camino family together.
3. I'm proud that I took so much from this amazing experience.

Gratitude

1. I'm grateful that my little Camino family spent one last night together.
2. I'm grateful for the amazing sunny weather we had today.
3. I'm grateful for the excellent albergue we stayed in tonight.

Day 34

FINISTERRE

rest day

Saturday, September 23rd, 2017

no time recorded

oday began with Jacob gently grabbing me by the kneecap and shaking me awake. As always, he was fully dressed, fully packed, and ready to go, and had awoken no one.

I arose, dressed, and hugged him goodbye, telling him how much of a pleasure it had been to share my Camino with him. We hugged several times.

"I'll miss you, Jacob."

"I'ma miss you, too." he replied, the only reference either one of us had made to the other in terms of how we felt about him.

He's gone off to spend four days hiking the 100 KM (62.14 mi.) long Camino Ingles.

"I thought I'd spend a few days laying on the beach," he said, "but I didn't come here to lay on the beach. I came here to walk. So that's what I'm gonna do!"

And that's just what he's doing. May the rhythmic "click-clack" of his walking sticks be motivating and inspiring to the few pilgrims he meets on the Ingles.

I tried to sleep again, but couldn't manage, so I lay in bed editing my photos for a while.

I heard Abigail and her parents shuffling about, so I went to return the socks I'd borrowed from Abigail's dad to him. We chatted briefly, and before long it was time to say goodbye, as they were moving on to Muxía.

I hugged Abigail several times, and, choked by my tears, couldn't really muster anything besides, "I'll miss you. Thank you."

She was surprisingly callous in a way. There was no sentimentality from her, really, which is unusual, I think, for a psychologist. All she said was, "ach, come here," the same way she's said to many animals along the way, including the goat from last night.

Strangely, I'm happy by how unaffected I was by her lack of sentimentality. I know we shared a special connection, and I know she would agree. We had a great time together, and genuinely care for one another.

The only overt indication she ever gave as to how she feels was when, in Lugo, full of wine and celebration, she was smoking a cigarette outside the bar, and reached over, grabbed my arm, and just said, excitedly, "Ach! Favorite!" Someone asked, "you mean Blake's your favorite?" to which she replied, "Yes! He's my favorite!" I just said nothing, knowing how unusual such brazen emotional outbursts were for her. I didn't want to draw attention to it. I just was glad for it.

But actions showed me she cares. Like when she arrived to A Fonsagrada ahead of me, and called to coordinate our finding of the albergue. She didn't find one of the three on her own, which she was more than capable of. She called, asked me what I thought of our options, and offered to wait at a cafe till I arrived and we found the place together. That's love, and I felt it.

I genuinely hope we meet again. I might make a trip to Copenhagen just for the purpose of having a laugh with her, and sooner than I would think.

As I stood there, staring at the sunrise through the hostel window, folding my laundry which I hoped after two hours in a dryer was bed bug free, sniveling and choking back tears, a hand was placed on my shoulder. I turned to find a beautiful woman, younger than me, but taller, with matronly curves and penetrating emerald-blue eyes wrapped in a flowing dress.

"Do you need anything?" She asked sweetly, softly.

"No...thank you so much, I'm fine," I said, tears rolling down my cheeks. "It's just very emotional, you know?"

She smiled. She did know. And I was touched by her kindness and calmed by her touch.

It was only around 9:00 at this point. Olivia and I spent the rest of the morning cafe hopping by the port, and sipping coffee between tears and laughs, and writing in our journals. We did this frequently throughout the Camino. We were journaling buddies. It made journaling even more enjoyable. It was such a lovely way to quietly enjoy each other's company. Writing silently next to one another, usually with beer or wine, and interrupting the other intermittently to discuss something our writing reminded us of, or just to take a little break.

Before leaving the hostel, Kyle stopped me. "Hey, Blake. Don't forget: enjoy this!"

"Enjoy what?"

"THIS. Where we are. This day. We came a long way to get here! Don't forget to feel good about it."

I was so thankful for this reminder. He may have misinterpreted my tears for bad sadness, not good sadness, but equally I needed to remember to feel the good of the moment, the pride and joy and excitement of a job very well done. So I spent the rest of the day crying with a smile.

After eating a massive salad for lunch, which Kyle and Olivia whipped up at the hostel, we headed to the beach where we stared in awe of the crashing Atlantic Ocean, far too cold for any of us to brave the water, and the fog on the horizon which slowly crept toward, up, and over the hills on the far right side of the beach, like an endless queue of ghostly ants clamoring over the hillside, covering it like a blanket.

I don't know if it was the warning Kyle had given me, or the joint he and I smoked on the beach, but I cried no more for the rest of the day. I just really enjoyed it.

We went back to town for a coffee and some grocery shopping before returning to the hostel, and heading back up to the lighthouse for the sunset. It was beautiful, but I was glad to have seen the sunset from the night before, which, because there was less cloud cover, Olivia and I agreed, was far more impressive.

Having smoked another joint and drank a beer while watching the sunset, I was happy to walk the 3 KM (1.86 mi.) back to town along the dark coastal road very slowly. I was struck by how happy I was to be walking, by how good it felt, from head to toe, by how connected it made me feel to my body. It was a pleasure to be walking after a day of not walking.

We went back to the hippie bar, where there was food, and ate a late dinner. The rest of the night various pilgrims we'd met along the way filtered in and out, and we were all quite happy, though it did lack the sheen of the night before, when Abigail and Jacob were there.

I went home around midnight. Olivia was shocked to see me leaving.

"But what's happened?! You never go home when there's still beer being drank!"

She was right, but I just thought I was ready to go home. So I left the crowd of acquaintances and headed back to the hostel, hoping with a fair amount of certainty that I had cut myself off in time to avoid a hangover. I didn't need that further complicating what is guaranteed to be a massively emotional day tomorrow, as we leave Finisterre, and I head back to Porto.

I bought my bus ticket to Porto today while Kyle and Olivia made lunch. It was funny that I didn't bother to look at hostels or even a map of the city. I'm usually a meticulous and very anxious planner of trips. But I feel confident that the Camino will, as it ever has, provide. I'll sort out hostels and a plan tomorrow. I may play tourist for a few days, or I may walk the Camino Portuguese. I haven't decided, but I figure at least one day in Porto is in order.

Olivia, as I was buying my bus ticket, flipped through the guidebook I had been given about the Camino Portugues by a pilgrim returning home. She had expressed interest in the Portugues as an option after finisterre.

"I have a question...But...how can I ask this?"

"Just ask, Olivia."

"Just ask?" I nodded. "Am I invited to come with you?"

"Of course! You can come with me to the end of the Earth, you don't have to ask."

"But maybe you want to be alone?"

"No, I don't need or want to be alone. I'd be happy to be with you. But I just don't know if I'll walk. I may not walk. I don't know." I spoke cautiously, carefully, because I'm still uncertain myself of what I'll do when I get there.

"Okay, I'll think about it." She said, and went to get ready.

I'd be thrilled for her company, though I do feel strangely comfortable, confident about going alone.

All my lovin',

- Blake.

Pride

1. I'm proud that I booked a bus ticket to Porto, and was completely unworried about the rest of the journey (hostel, times, neighborhoods, etc.)

2. I'm proud that I am perfectly at ease with crying in public and in private.

3. I'm proud that I had so many people to be thrilled to have met, and sorrowful to be leaving.

Gratitude

1. I'm grateful for the excellent sunrise we had today, and the excellent sunset.

2. I'm grateful for having had such a nice rest day with Olivia and Kyle.

3. I'm grateful for having Olivia as a journaling partner.

Day 35

FISTERRA → PORTO, PORTUGAL

*S*itting in a trendy bar surrounded by hip young people sipping craft beers while the speakers blast music from Electronic/ House, to Prince, Billy Idol to Beach House to Tears for Fears, it is clear that I'm not in Spain anymore.

Porto, I have gathered in the three hours I've been here, feels like a cross between Copenhagen, Berlin, and Austin. Olivia and Kyle both raved about it. I'm sceptical, but only because I can't convince myself I don't want to be on the Camino. Still, I'm happy to be here if only because I proved I could get off the Camino, which felt as uncertain as getting on it in the first place.

I was quite proud of the calmness and confidence with which I arrived. Travel always makes me very anxious, but I felt perfectly fine when I arrived here, and made it to my hostel with my handwritten directions. It's a bit redundant to copy directions from my phone to paper, I know, but it helps me get my bearings better, and makes me look up at the city to find the street names rather than down at my phone to see when the blue dot tells me I should turn.

At the hostel, I spoke openly, easily, offhandedly with my four roommates, devoid of the choking anxiety which usually keeps me

silent and shadow-like in hostels full of strangers. I even got them laughing, and they invited me to a jazz concert they'll attend this evening.

I came to a local bar as soon as I arrived to have a beer and write. I'd hoped I would cry, but the tears always wait for the most inappropriate time to start welling up.

Today was a day full of tears of all kinds. It was an overwhelming state of emotion which I experienced all morning; a state of many emotions at once: grateful, thankfulness, love, pride, sorrow, exhaustion, energized, content, confused, sadness, happiness, and a host of others which made brief cameos on the stage of my heart. And, in this heightened state of emotional uncertainty, I was brought to tears at the most minor hint of sentimentality, except when I was alone and could really let the floodgates open, a mission I tried to carry out several times in the last two days, to no avail.

Olivia told me that she's never seen a man cry before, and if she did, it was because someone had died! She said seeing me cry just made her cry instantly, but that it was good for her to see a man cry. She saw plenty of it today.

This morning I awoke easily, readily, at 7:00, having gone to bed with a heart enriched by a day well lived, and having slept the slumber of a man truly content.

Initially I planned to spend the two hours before the bus left sitting by the port, sipping coffee, crying, and waiting. But after a shower, my first morning shower in 34 days, a luxury I most enjoyed, and eating a breakfast of oats and yogurt, I had another idea.

At the bar the night before, Gabriel described to me a past tradition of pilgrims in which in order to get the Compostela, pilgrims first had to arrive at Finisterre, collect sea shells from the shore, and return to Santiago and show their seashells as proof that they'd made it to the sea. This is something many pilgrims still do, and I thought it might provide me some closure, not to mention, a secluded beach from which to watch the sunrise and weep with the reckless abandon my swollen heart yearned for.

I strolled the 500 meters (546.81 yd.) to the beach in the dim light of dawn and picked at the sand, plucking a shell from the surf, then another, then discarding one for a cleaner, more colorful one. I did this for about 20 minutes while strolling down the deserted beach until I had a few, some for friends, one for Olivia and Kyle, and one for myself, all while the light of the Sun began to pierce the frigid grey clouds over the mountains across the bay and cast glorious, sharp, hot colors across the ceiling of the clouds in soft, haphazard patterns. I stared at the little shells, and thought about what they symbolized, for me, and for my journey. Here I held in my hand the physical proof of the completion of a journey for which I have no words adequate to describe its significance, its power, its place in my life. I thought about it for a moment, and felt the weight of the shells in my hand, strangely light, yet so charged with meaning.

"Thank you," I said to no one. "This is perhaps the most significant thing I've ever done. Thank you."

I sat on a tiny fishing boat parked on the beach and watched the Sun rise majestically through the clouds, over the mountains, chasing the dark of night away, and replacing it with colors impossible to reproduce in word or art, as the gulls danced wildly over the water, and the small waves washed ashore, drowning out all noise and thought; bringing with them more tokens of a life-changing journey which lie in wait to be plucked from the sand by overwhelmed pilgrims to come. I tried hard to calm my wandering mind; to stay present and let this moment, completely my own, wash over me.

Still, as ever, the tears didn't come when I most wanted to cry them. It's hard to know when you've watched the best part of a sunrise, so I sat until my feet asked to leave and began walking back across the beach. In the sand, pointing against the direction I was currently walking, were a single set of footprints in the sand; my footprints, that unmistakable pigeon toe, those defining geometric shapes in the soles of my ridiculous trail running shoes.

These were the marks of the feet that had carried me so far, so reliable, so dependable, each step placed with care and purpose; these were the marks of a journey completed, made all the more poignant by the fact that I was now, for the first time, retracing my steps, not to find the right path, or to go out of my way to see a sight located off the Camino. This time, I was retracing my steps to go home. Here, on this beach, truly, finally, lay my 0 KM mark. And of course now, as I write this, at a table in the Portuguese sun at a local cafe, now the tears come at the thought of the finale I found so unexpectedly on that beach.

Y así, se cambió una vida entera.

Olivia and I found our way to a coffee shop near the bus stop where we sat crying and laughing together, she far more gracefully than I, her tears never breaking the barrier of her eyeliner, while mine poured forth, accompanied by quiet snivelling, a runny nose, and a quivering, froggy voice.

Of course, I think crying is beautiful, and I'm unashamed to cry in public, as Olivia noted. It's a sign that a human is experiencing something so laden with emotional experience that the body just doesn't know how to react, so it cries. And it feels so good. And whether they are tears of joy, as mine were, or tears of sorrow, no one should be banished to cry silently in a bathroom, as we so often are, experiencing some emotional turmoil so beautiful, so meaningful, in the same 3x3 cubicle where we evacuate our bowels, often while someone else is doing just that mere inches away. So I cry, with pride, in public.

We were lucky and got a direct bus back to Santiago at 9:30. Olivia lay her head on my shoulder and slept a while. It was lovely. It's such a sign of security and safety and comfort to sleep next to someone, and to sleep on them even more. I was glad for the sign of friendship, and for the human contact, of which I had far too little throughout my Camino, and which was perhaps the only thing I missed more than a good night of wakeless sleep.

Back in Santiago, Kyle, Olivia, and I got a coffee, and I let Kyle book me a hostel in Porto, which is actually very nice.

Kyle then went to get his Compostela while Olivia and I hunted down postcards and had a beer in a cafe while we wrote them, and, of course, cried some more together, laughing at what the few people around us and the waiters must think of us, and what stories they must be inventing for us, and how silly we both were crying at that table.

On the bus I asked Olivia what she'd do after Santiago, and she decided that she would stay in Spain. She told me that although she felt welcome to come, and although the Camino Portugues really called to her, she didn't want to come because her intuition told her I needed to be alone; to go alone. I told her that she shouldn't change her plan based on me, and that we could sit on opposite sides of the bus, or get separate hostels if she thought I should be alone, but that she should go to Portugal if that's what she wanted. She wasn't sure about it, and I think she didn't want to walk alone, which she had told me about why she didn't want to go on the Camino Ingles. I think she wanted me to say, "Olivia, definitely come with me!" but I wasn't, and am still not, sure I wanted to walk, and I didn't want to drag her here without knowing 100% that I would walk as well. So perhaps it was the hesitance with which I said she should come that kept her from joining.

I told her again in the restaurant where we were writing, and she said she was leaving the door open if only to make saying goodbye easier.

I wrote a postcard to myself which I'll seal, and leave sealed, forgotten, until a day comes when I'm met with something of seemingly impossible odds, an idea I'd taken from Olivia.

Kyle met us when he was done, and we took a walk to the cathedral where we drank a beer and watched the pilgrims coming in, hoping to relive that moment a bit. Before long it was time for me to head to my bus. I was crying, and Kyle said, "Drink it in, Blake." So I smiled, and started to hug them several times in turn, unable to say more than "thank you," I'll miss you," and, "come visit." They were both equally as speechless. Olivia and I hugged tightly, deeply, and with all the love in our hearts. It was beautiful and difficult.

As I walked away, Kyle said, "Love you, brother," and I answered, "I love you, too." and I think I added, "Buen Camino!" and walked to the bus station.

I boarded the bus after waiting about 15 minutes for it to arrive, and moments before the bus departed, I caught a glimpse of a shock of blonde hair and a bright orange jacket moving down the aisle toward me. It was Olivia. I couldn't believe it.

"You're coming to Portugal!" I said, overjoyed.

"No. My albergue is here, and I couldn't resist." She hugged me.

"You sure you aren't coming tomorrow?" I asked.

"Yeah," she replied, and hugged me again before turning and exiting the bus. I was shocked, and touched, and saddened, surprisingly saddened that she wouldn't be coming. I suppose I should have known when she tried to give me her walking sticks when we said goodbye at the cathedral. Her Camino is finished. And when the bus closed its door and began pulling away from the station, so was mine.

I looked everywhere for her, just to wave goodbye one more time, but she was nowhere to be found.

All my lovin',

- Blake.

Day 35

Pride

1. I'm proud to have made such good friends on the Camino
2. I'm proud I immediately made friends at the hostel, and spoke with confidence, ease.
3. I'm proud that I've chosen alone time for writing and reflecting.

Gratitude

1. I'm so grateful for the sunrise I saw this morning.
2. I'm grateful Kyle and Olivia were there to bring my Camino to its official close.
3. I'm grateful for my camino, and all that came with it.

Epilogue

Day 36

PORTO, PORTUGAL

Monday, September 25th, 2017

no time recorded

No journal entry written.

Day 31

PORTO → PÓVOA DE VARZIM

37 km / 22.99 mi.

Tuesday, September 26th, 2017

no time recorded

No journal entry written.

Day 38

PÓVOA DE VARZIM → COIMBRA

.

Wednesday, September 27th, 2017

no time recorded

I awoke a few minutes before my alarm went off at 7:00.

I slept beautifully, deeply. I felt rested. So rested I paused for a moment to debate whether I'd made the right decision. I would almost certainly be plunged back into the realm of insomnia; into nights of sleeplessness, tossing, turning, and the throbbing in my knee. Was it wise? Was it what I actually wanted? Squeezing into a sleeping bag sure to induce a fit of itching via the certainty I had of sharing that cloth space with many-legged nocturnal parasites? I paused. The duvet, faux down, lay heavily, softly, upon me, wrapping me in comfort and security. I hadn't felt this comfortable in weeks. How could I walk away from this?

Quickly, and with purpose. That's how.

I ate a big breakfast knowing I would need the calories. I was in no rush. The cathedral didn't open until 9:00, and I'd need the stamp before leaving Porto, so I ate slowly, savoring the cereal and milk, the toast and store bought plastic cheese. I wouldn't have a breakfast which included juice for another short while. Better drink two cups, then.

I said a brief goodbye to Elise, a Kiwi with whom I had spent the previous evening having drinks and dinner. She was smiling and unsurprised to see me going.

I grabbed my walking sticks, sitting idly in a basket by the hostel's door for the last 36 hours, strapped on my rucksack, and hit the pavement, marching toward the yellow arrows I saw the day before, which taunted me, beckoning me toward the cathedral, and from there, back to the river on Porto's Southern border, and from there to the Atlantic Coast, where the Camino Portugues leads all the way back to Santiago.

It was funny how the sticks, at first awkward and cumbersome, and the rucksack, initially heavy and restrictive, felt so natural, so comforting. I felt a wave of relief as I began striding toward my destination, sticks click-clacking on the cobbled sidewalk, all of my possessions sealed in a bag squeezing me from behind. Everything I needed, and the road under my feet. I was happy; excited.

I stopped at a tiny cafe on a sunny plaza where I had done a fair bit of sitting, writing, and people watching already. The view was good, the service friendly, and the coffee cheap and rich.

At the cathedral I smiled as another stamp was added to my Pilgrim's credential, then crossed the Dom Luis I bridge, strolling 45 meters (49.21 yd.) over the water of the Douro River, into Vila Nova de Gaia, in order to get a view of Porto, tiny doll houses rubbing shoulders, all stacked up into a pile of pastel reds, blues, and yellows, bathed in the morning sunlight.

It was so beautiful, and the vibe of the city so familiar and charming, I wondered again if I was making the right choice. It was a fleeting thought.

Descending some narrow, winding streets, I crossed back over the Douro River via the underside of the bridge only a few meters above the water, and began walking along the riverbank, flocks of tourists already doing the same, and began walking the Camino Portugues.

While I had thoroughly enjoyed my day in Porto, I just couldn't shake the feeling that I should be on the Camino instead. It felt wrong, unnatural, to spend so much time sitting, strolling, idly filling time with photographs and viewpoints spread across the city. I missed the structure of the Camino, the simplicity of it, and found myself almost overwhelmed at the prospect of having to find ways to fill the days spent as a normal tourist. And I missed the kilometers of uninterrupted, brisk, purposeful walking. I craved it. So when faced with the choice, another few days playing tourist in Portugal, or filling a few more days as a pilgrim on the Camino, walking was a clear winner.

I had neither the desire nor the time to make it all the way back to Santiago. For that I would need between seven and ten days, and I only had four days of walking if I wanted to spend two days in Lisbon, from where my flight to Berlin would depart. That would give me enough time to walk the 100 KM (62.14 mi.) along the Atlantic coast all the way to the Spanish border in four stages of about 25 - 35 KM (15.53 - 21.75 mi.) each. Adding 100 KM (62.15 mi.) to my journey would guarantee that I would have covered a total distance of 1000 KM (621.37 mi.), and while a totally arbitrary figure, I must admit the number was nice and round, and very enticing.

So that was my plan. But of course, 25 KM (15.53 mi.) per day was very short, so I decided to try to knock it out in 3 days, and then take a bus to Lisbon, where I'd have two full days to acclimate myself to civilian life.

One last reason for being happy to return to the Camino is how cheap the Camino is. €5.00 for the albergue, €3.00 on Camino snacks, €10.00 for a pilgrim menu, two stops at a cafe/bar for maybe €7.00, and the day costs less than €25.00, which is less expensive than my normal daily life.

All total, the return to the Camino was exciting. The first part of the day flew by. My legs felt stronger than ever after the tiny respite, and I was simply flying along the cobblestone sidewalk bordering the sea.

By noon I had walked nearly 15 KM (9.32 mi.), not bad considering I didn't leave the Dom Luis bridge until just before 10:00. I was surprised by the number of pilgrims I found myself passing. There were far more than I had anticipated, but then I had read that the Portuguese Camino has become the second most popular among the Caminos, second only after the French Way. I stopped briefly at the tourist office and got another stamp and another map. I didn't really need the map, as I had an app on my phone for the Camino Portugues, but the woman was so kind and filled the map with helpful information including distances from city to city that I didn't want to turn it away.

I continued on a little way and felt my stomach grumbling. It was already time for a pit stop. I kept my eyes peeled for a cafe, and couldn't believe my luck when I saw a sandwich board offering tortilla, the carbo-loaded, protein packed Spanish-style omelette, which had become a staple for all of us on the Camino.

I sat and had a piece of tortilla and a coffee. Sitting alone at that table, a day full of walking ahead of me, a day devoid of distraction or complication, I felt at peace. In fact, I felt at home. The tortilla was so good I had another piece before I headed off toward the beach, where another 22 KM (13.67 mi.) of walking awaited me.

Without trying to diminish the joy of being back on the camino, I must admit that the Camino Portugues had certainly left something to be desired. Firstly, the going was flat. Completely flat. I shouldn't have been surprised by this, as I was walking directly along the coast, which tends to be...sea-level. But all the same, the simplicity and repetition of each step left my joints hurting, and my heart yearning for a bit more excitement.

Additionally, the entire way consists of an incredibly long boardwalk. Impressive as it is, and thankful as I was not to have to walk in the sand, it felt a bit like cheating. The bounce of the planks beneath my feet were a welcome change to the pounding of the stone sidewalks leading out of Porto, but they were no substitute for the softened trails that led through the Primitivo.

While I felt genuinely joyful to be walking again, I had hoped I would be walking in more isolation. The entire 37 KM (22.99 mi.) I would cover today were bordered on at least one side with strips of apartments, shops, or busy roads. I hadn't quite found the serenity I had hoped for.

Lastly, and most detrimentally to the day on the Camino, there was the "Ocean Layer," which is apparently the term used to describe the incredibly thick fog which sits atop the water, unmoving and unyielding. It lay so thickly on the ground as to render the entire scene like something out of a post-apocalyptic dystopian film, in which the world is always inexplicably draped in fog, and all the world is viewed through a prism of silhouettes.

I could hear the ocean crashing into the beach ten meters (10.94 yd.) to my left, but could scarcely see it. I could make out conversations and heavy feet striking the boardwalk in front and behind me, but couldn't make out the origin of their providence. I could tell the Sun above was strong and bright, the sky blue and wide, but was shielded from such celestial delights, my world reduced to a colorless, horizonless bubble 10 meters (10.94 yd.) in diameter where everything was a fuzzy shade of grey.

With little to grab my attention externally, my thoughts turned inward. Before I knew it, I found myself reminiscing about the incredible journey I had recently completed; the people, places, and experiences I had recently come to know. Gently, my thoughts meandred to that first day, when I stepped, stiff and exhausted and nervous, off the bus in Bayonne. I began to relive that first day, remembering as many details as I could: the weather, the events that passed the time, How I was feeling, what I was thinking, where I was heading.

My thoughts meandered, carried me along what my memory believed to be the journey from Bayonne to Irún, and the time that passed from the train ride, to bedtime, my first night sleeping on the Camino.

In my mind's eye, I relived that first day, from waking and packing, to walking with Leo all the way to San Sebastián, the swim on the beach, the laughter with strangers, the desperate search for a kebab, the sleepless night, the morning shuffle out the door.

Just like the physical act of walking the Camino, once I started, I couldn't stop thinking about my trip. For the next three hours, I walked through the grey world, the Ocean crashing ashore to my left, reliving in as much detail every leg of the journey that had brought me to the Portuguese coast. I laughed aloud. I cried. I marched in silent reverence to the literal beat of the walking I was doing in my head.

Day by day passed heavily across my mind until finally I relived that invigorating and heartbreaking moment when Olivia climbed aboard my bus in Santiago just to say goodbye one last time.

As the tears ran down my face, and my heart swelled with emotion, I felt an overwhelming sense of relief. A weightlessness came over me. I felt relaxed in a way I hadn't expected. And just like that, I knew I was finished, I was done. I was ready to finally leave the Camino.

I don't know how I knew it, but I did. I was finished. My Camino had ended. I felt like Forrest Gump, who, after running coast to coast across The United States, much to the dismay of his followers, suddenly stops, turns, and says, "I think I'll go home now." He just knew he was done. And so did I.

I have come to believe that the feeling I had in Porto of just needing to be on the Camino was a symptom of not having taken the time to reflect and pay my respects to what was one of the most transformational experiences of my life.

In our busy world, we are often thinking several steps ahead, so that when one experience ends we already have a backlog of new events, experiences, and obligations which we feel responsible for attending to immediately. It is so easy to ignore the act of stopping, breathing, and reflecting upon the miracles of our everyday lives, including even our greatest accomplishments.

I think that nagging urge to keep walking was my very overwhelmed psyche begging for a breath, for a moment of pause and reflection which such weighty life experience merits; necessitates.

By reliving the Camino in my head, I believe I was unwittingly reflecting upon my journey, and thus inadvertently processing the emotion and experience and giving my psyche the chance it needed to process and digest and file it all away for safekeeping; to organize everything I had recently lived for easy retrieval at a later date when my search for an answer leads me to my past experiences and lessons.

After processing the shock of this sudden inner peace, I decided that I would stay one last night in an albergue, and head back to Porto the next day, and from there to some other place on my way down to Lisbon.

Not long after, the Ocean Layer began to show cracks where blue sky could be seen. Little by little it began to make its way slowly out to sea, inch by inch, revealing a bit more of the sky, scenery, and city until it eventually yielded completely, leaving me bathed in sunlight and the vibrant colors of the Portuguese tiles covering the tiny building and apartments I walked past. That last hour was a delight.

The city I stopped in, Póvoa de Varzim, is a small beach city, quaint, pretty, probably fairly uneventful. The albergue was practically empty, and was one of the nicer albergues I stayed in.

I eventually bought a beer and headed to the beach where I enjoyed one last sunset on the Camino, lying prostrate in the grainy sand, alone apart from a middle aged couple who spent so much time and energy taking selfies, I reckon they never saw the sunset with their naked eyes.

I later went to a restaurant where I had a Franceshina, a Portuguese specialty, in a restaurant full of Portuguese people eating Francesinhas and watching a soccer match.

As I ate, I planned my next moves:

- 2 days in the university city of Coimbra
- 2 days in Lisbon
- Home to Berlin

Upon returning to the albergue I drank a beer and chatted with two other pilgrims before showering and going to bed.

When I left the albergue in the morning, I left my walking sticks in a bucket by the door in the hope that they might serve some pilgrim passing through.

Of course the weather was splendid: cool, not a cloud in the sky. I was almost tempted to keep going, one more day. Almost.

I stopped at a tiny cafe in a quiet plaza and had a tearful cup of coffee, enveloped in a whirlwind of emotions. Then I got up and got on the train back to Porto.

All my lovin',

- Blake.

Pride

1. I'm proud that I took such a thorough account of my Camino via my journal

2. I'm proud I told my mom to get her passport ready, and that I want her and Bruce to come visit me.

3. I'm proud of the calm and ease with which I traveled to Coimbra today.

Gratitude

1. I'm grateful for the wonderful weather I've had today.

2. I'm grateful for how wonderful my hostel is.

3. I'm grateful to have Kyle's words about learning to chill ringing in my ears. It's helping me more easily pass the time in this small city, and I think will be a lesson I'll carry with me for a long time.

Afterword

Deja Vu

I've definitely experienced this before, and I could swear it was just yesterday. Here I sit, once again, staring at my computer screen, a little numb, enveloped in a state of disbelief. Only instead of the neon lines of incomprehensible computer code, my laptop is filled with row upon coherent row of the black and white text comprising my typed Camino journal. These simple lines, though far easier to decipher, have proven no less thought-provoking than the HTML and JavaScript from which I once attempted to extract some semblance of meaning.

Can it really be that 854 full days have passed since I left that plaza in Póvoa de Varzim, and in so doing took my leave of the Camino de Santiago? What's to be gleaned today from these words I wrote 2 years,

4 months, and 2 days ago? What lessons does the version of myself that existed an unfathomable 1,229,760 minutes ago have to impart upon the version of myself that sits here today; upon anyone who might have found themselves perusing his emotionally laden thoughts?

So much has changed in the nearly 74 million seconds that have ticked silently past since I abandoned my walking sticks and donned those horrifying orange trail runners for the last time. And yet, frustratingly, so much feels exactly the same. Enough that I find myself wondering: What did I actually learn on that 950 KM (590.30 mile) journey? What did I manage to bring back with me apart from a battered compilation of jumbled ruminations, a throbbing knee, and an egregious farmer's tan? How did those tentative plans and naive epiphanies pan out? What would that hopeful pilgrim, hair dyed blonde by the sun and heart bursting with a sense of accomplishment, have to say about where I've led him and what I've done with all his musings on how better to approach the Camino that is life?

Hitting the Ground Running

Pilgrim Blake would certainly be happy to know that in the immediate aftermath of my return to Berlin, things went exactly to plan. Within a matter of days, in a manner so calm and optimistic as to render pre-Camino Blake speechless, I gathered all the necessary paperwork (3 binders full) and ticked all the bureaucratic boxes necessary to convince the German state to award me with a highly coveted unrestricted work visa. I never thought the prospect of being allowed to clean toilets or wait tables would give me such a thrill! For the first time in my immigrant life I was liberated from the condition that I provide an incontrovertible and substantial benefit to my host-country. With the addition of this flashy bureaucratic sticker to my passport, I became empowered with free rein to earn money however I saw fit.

So, naturally, much to the chagrin of every xenophobe in existence, I went immediately and proudly to the unemployment office to apply for benefits. After working diligently in an office for three and a half years paying into the social welfare system, I figured I had earned a few months of government support while I took some time to stoke the embers of creative energy - which my day job had all but extinguished - still glowing softly within me.

With this artist's subsidy, as I liked to refer to it, firmly in hand, I set to work on my guitar, devoting myself fully to self-producing a homemade EP years in the making. Those five DIY tracks, appropriately titled *Turn the Page*, represented a chance to let go of the past and move forward afresh. With every strum of the guitar, with every falsetto note I belted, I was tearing eagerly into the next chapter of my life with the certainty that its fresh, unmarked pages brimmed with the prospect of new beginnings. On a cold, wet December evening in a vibrant, smokey Berlin bar called "Radio," I played a concert to an audience of my incredibly supportive friends to celebrate my 31st birthday, as well as the release of *Turn the Page* and my first-ever music video.

With the flame of creativity well-kindled and burning brightly, and, with an inordinate amount of free time thanks to my unemployment benefits, I threw myself into a handful of new projects, still nourished by a seemingly indefatigable spring of positivity and hope left over from the Camino. Delving into the unforgotten cache of songs I wrote in my time as a struggling singer/songwriter in Austin, Texas, I set almost immediately to recording a second self-released EP, *This Place is Not My Home*.

While *Turn the Page* contemplated what it takes to leave the past behind and move forward, *This Place is Not My Home* explores the difficulty of moving forward when a lifelong search for belonging leads right back to the starting point. These old songs took on a new weight in light of my recent spiritual voyage focused on introspection and settling my combative ego. They suddenly reminded me that I could only hope to find the resolution to external stressors in my life by looking within myself.

Simultaneously, as I chipped away at *This Place is Not My Home* track by track, I registered for an intensive German class. The course, paid for by the German state (naturally), brought structure, human contact, and a sense of momentum to what could easily have spiraled into months of critical isolation. Instead of literally hiding under the sheets from the threat of an alarmingly fruitless job search and the gnawing sensation of wasted potential, I spent four days during every week of that abusively cold winter in solidarity with a room full of foreigners whose backgrounds were as diverse as their mother tongues. Together, we struggled to cram German's infamously rigid and complex grammar rules into our heads along with an ever-expanding list of vocabulary whose connection and resemblance to our own native languages faded with each passing lesson. Thankfully, I passed the end-of-course exam, with the highest score in the class no less. The B2 Level certificate I received stands as incontrovertible evidence that I, Blake Farha, speak German confidently, with a proficiency adequate for both a German-speaking workplace and the permanent residence visa I set my sights on.

As I promised myself back on the Camino, the time not spent studying German or shouting into a microphone I reserved for "making myself available to new, unthought of opportunities to which my fears have blinded me…" With nothing else to do one Thursday night in November and in need of some human contact after a day spent locked in my makeshift bedroom studio, I stumbled into an improv comedy jam at a local bar where anyone could sign up and get on stage. Although I had never done improv before, I remembered loving the hilarious improv television show hosted by Drew Carey, "Whose Line is it Anyway?" and figured I'd give it a shot. Stepping onto the stage that night, I became instantly hooked.

Signing up for my first improv comedy course, I could never have imagined that, before long, improv would become the single focal point of my entire life and almost immediately lead me to my first entrepreneurial endeavor (considering one doesn't count my stint as a semi-starving musician). It didn't take me long to see that the skillset an improvisor uses onstage to create engaging scenes has immense value off-stage. Together with a friend I set out to spread The Improv Mindset, using improv comedy as a context for teaching soft skills, hard skills, and everything in between. Within two months of hatching this idea, we booked our first corporate client, and within nine months we were both able to survive (just barely) purely on the money we were earning with our improv workshops.

In the two years since we embarked upon our improvised entrepreneurial journey, we managed to accidentally create a tiny ecosystem with The Improv Mindset at its core. We wrote and published "The Improv Manifesto" which forms the backbone of everything we believe, in terms of how one can harness the power of improv principles to live a brighter, fuller life. We've given our workshops to companies like Google, Babbel, N26, and Axel-Springer/ Porsche in four different countries. Our podcast, "Improvise Till You Make It!," has reached a modest audience in 29 countries. The offerings of our 8-week private classes have expanded to four different courses, and our student body continues to grow while our weekly drop-in class constantly puts new people in touch with improv for the first time. Our improv team, Skeleton Brains, won a local competition, and our bi-weekly show regularly draws a large, boisterous audience. I play on two other improv teams, one of which (Rollercoasters) won the audience award for Best New Format at the Warsaw Improv Festival in 2019. At the moment I find myself on stage as many as four times per week, performing in one show or another. With all of these moving parts, our small business miraculously, and to my regular disbelief, continues to pay the bills. I dare say that it even shows promise for growth and prosperity in the near future.

While I've dedicated a huge part of my time since leaving the Camino to work and business, the last couple of years have also been peppered with plenty of smaller adventures and relevant life-events.

After a brief stint in physical therapy and months of patiently reteaching myself how to properly climb stairs, my left knee has returned to a state of perfect health.

I've upgraded from that much sought-after unrestricted work visa and, as of September 2019, I'm officially a German permanent resident. I can live and work comfortably here for the rest of my life, unburdened by the existential threat of a rejected visa application and its accompanying request to vacate the premises of the Federal Republic of Germany.

I produced and self-published this book and the accompanying audiobook at the same time as I started working as a narrator and voice actor for the English arm of the German international public broadcaster, Deutsche Welle.

Somewhere along the way I started learning the piano and wrote another full album's worth of songs which I hope to begin recording after publishing this book.

Although my parents, unfortunately, have yet to make the journey across the pond, I did have the immense pleasure of hosting my sister for two weeks. A glorious Berlin summer provided us with unprecedented good weather in which to spend our days basking in the sunshine by the shores of lakes, and our evenings hanging out in parks with my friends.

For a total of three weeks on two separate occasions, I lived in a tour bus and traveled all over France slinging merchandise for PuppetMastaz, a raucous hip-hop group comprised of rapping puppets.

I spent nearly a month living in two separate off-grid communities in Portugal. Mountain views greeted me as I crawled out of my tent every morning. I spent my days harvesting olives, chopping down trees, building houses by hand, and my nights preparing communal dinners and singing around bonfires beneath starry skies.

For two weeks I volunteered to work in a nudist community in Southern France. I learned how arduous, thankless, and shockingly unprofitable operating a small-scale ecological organic farm is, while simultaneously experiencing the endless joys of wandering through a forest wearing only my birthday suit.

I gave up drinking alcohol for an entire year, and I would recommend that everyone do the same.

So there it is: the instagram-worthy version of the past two years, four months, and two days. I must admit, this patchwork summary paints a marvelous picture of a lost soul finally finding his voice replete with any number of details deserving of a like, a share, and maybe even the odd emoji-filled comment. Reading it over once again, I find myself nodding in recognition, eyebrows fully raised, lips pursed and curled down at the corners, like a proud father who tragically never learned how to express his feelings. It's been, without a doubt, a whirlwind of discovery, adventure, and positive momentum.

The Honeymoon Ends

Why, then, do I have my doubts that the Blake who wrote this journal would be anything less than chuffed at where I've taken him in the time since he passed me the proverbial torch? How come I find myself wondering if I managed to actually learn anything from all that walking, journaling, and soul seeking? Because I have a dirty little secret: the path on which I have found myself, with all of its unexpected twists and unforeseen turns, has been anything but a walk in the park. Like any instagram page worth its salt, this well-tailored narrative has been manicured to reveal only the shimmering outcomes and sparkling accomplishments which stand as checkpoints on the Camino I've walked since Santiago. All the unglamorous parts of the journey, no matter how consequential, have been tossed out like so much unwanted litter fated to lie neglected in a ditch by the side of the road.

On Day 29, after the Pilgrim Mass ended, I decided, to the joy and astonishment of the lonely priest reading intently in the confessional booth, to receive confession. My reasons for kneeling and laying open my sins in the house of God bear repeating:

> I didn't confess because I wanted forgiveness from a God I don't believe in. I confessed because [...] [s]ymbols have meaning and power. And this was my symbol.

> I wasn't speaking to a priest, or to God. I was speaking to myself, to the universe. I was admitting openly that I have wronged myself, and in doing so, making a vow, outloud, into a void, an energy, a world of spirituality, that a transformation has taken place; that I won't continue a life of cruelty to myself; that I will love myself, and in doing so, as the priest suggested, better serve the universe in which I live, of which I am a part as beautiful, unique, and valuable as anything else within it.

> Y así, se cambió una vida entera. [And like that, an entire life changed.]

> Day 29

"And like that, an entire life changed." Unfortunately, as much as I would love to whole-heartedly believe it, I have ample reason to call the veracity of that statement into question. It's certainly true that I could never have predicted the shape my life has taken since I returned to Berlin. However, it cannot be denied that an alarming number of the cracks in the foundation upon which that life has been built remain unrepaired and routinely threaten to bring everything constructed precariously upon them toppling down.

At its worst, the trembling beneath the surface, perhaps unnoticed by the casual onlooker, culminates in a deafening rumble compelling me to genuinely consider ending it all.

Suicide. Here stands perhaps the strongest evidence against the proclamation that I returned from the Camino a changed man. On Day 7 of the Camino, I boldly exalted, "I feel I have genuinely turned a corner, and feel as though, come what may, on my new path, the potential for the viability of, the potential for resorting to suicide, has vanished around the bend I have left behind, as I head for greener pastures beyond my new horizon." Were it not for the fact that I sincerely meant every word of it when I wrote it, this would be called out in court as a bold-faced lie.

The high of the Camino resonated within me for months. Propelled through a miserable winter by unprecedented amounts of hope and positivity with which the journey filled me, I truly hit the ground running back in Berlin. I have perhaps never felt so creative, so productive, and so optimistic about the future.

Slowly, but surely, however, bad mental habits crept back in. Mired in an environment of growing uncertainty as I began building my own small business and with the funds in my "artist subsidy" rapidly dwindling, I found myself once again flirting with demons I thought I'd all but gotten over. Like detrimental lovers from the past nearly forgotten, their familiarity comforted me, wooed me, seduced me in a time of immense vulnerability until at last I crumbled into their arms allowing myself to be whisked away, ever faster, down the steep slope of depression. It was less than a year before I had the first of many breakdowns which paved the way for those menacing suicidal thoughts to come slithering back into my head where they continue to lurk in the shadows, unnoticed until the screaming instant they decide to sink their fangs in.

I set out on the Camino to vanquish many of the selfsame demons, yet their continued existence gives them license to charm the serpents of self-destruction from their den and casts a heavy shadow on the growth and perspective I believed myself to have achieved throughout the course of my pilgrimage.

Principal among these impediments to inner peace: Perfectionism. As early as Day -2, I call this issue out by name. "My perfectionism wants everything to have an end to justify itself, and rejects the notion that some things, maybe most things, are in fact an end in themselves, or at least should be allowed the opportunity to be." While I managed to quell this feeling over and over again on the Camino, eventually this insidious tar began seeping into my thoughts. From the speed with which my business grew, to the amount of laughter my improv team wrested from the audience; from the location of my new apartment to the amount of sunshine falling on my patch of lakeshore, a slew of what should have been proud achievements and precious moments became irrevocably sullied by Perfectionism's heavy black film and deemed unfit for an ego which esteems itself so highly. I once again began to reject everything I was doing and everything I had as "not being good enough," and I soon found myself in a place where I felt contented with almost nothing in what others surely see as a vibrant, active life. I had won the battle with this beast on the way to Santiago, but, at least until very recently, it appeared to have won the war.

Allowing Perfectionism to tote me deeper and deeper into the forest of self-doubt, I suddenly found myself once again contending with one of its most trusted accomplices: Isolation. Increasingly convinced that nothing I could accomplish would merit the recognition I so crave, I reverted to setting maniacally high standards for the amount and quality of work I must produce, depriving myself of a healthy social life. I might go days without having a real conversation, literally locking myself in my bedroom-studio or spending entire weekends behind my computer screen simply because I'd been so busy "working" I'd forgotten to make plans, or because I rejected plans in lieu of "getting something productive done." Those days of chatting with every stranger I came across on the Camino vanished as I rapidly drew into myself. The feelings of inadequacy spawned by Perfectionism persuaded me I was unworthy of talking to what I perceived to be the endlessly amazing, productive, successful people surrounding me. I went from being the life of the party to an inconsistently present wallflower until I could no longer hide from myself or others the crushing social anxiety I almost completely abandoned en route to Santiago.

By the time my ego began mimicking the cruelty it learned from Perfectionism, I had already cut myself off from most of my support network. Few people could even witness its incredible brutality, and even fewer could do anything against the ferocious attacks taking place behind the walls of my consciousness. Self-Loathing had let itself in, plopped down on the couch, put its feet up on the coffee table, and cracked open a beer. The blossoming relationship with myself which began to bud on the Camino quickly descended back into the helpless child and the abusive alcoholic I wrote about on that beach in Deba three days into the journey. I again became my own worst enemy.

These three forces, Perfectionism, Isolation, and Self-Loathing, all of which I intentionally set out to combat, and about which I wrote nearly 150 pages, blew in from beyond the horizon and coalesced into a tempest through which I could no longer navigate. Working too hard and too much led to both literal and metaphorical isolation. Isolation deepened my feelings of inadequacy and fueled my self-loathing. To flee said self-loathing, I overpacked my schedule with projects, meetings, and goals. The pressure of meeting these demands as efficiently and effectively as possible squeezed nearly all the joy out of my daily existence, leaving only enough space for an electric stress and the knowledge that tomorrow would feel exactly the same. Around and around it went, until this toxic concoction congealed into a poisonous hopelessness which I have fluctuated between indulging in and having the strength to resist for the past two years.

Occasionally I'll hit a target so satisfying, or take a trip so enriching and so distant from my stressors and triggers (like when I spent some time off grid in Portugal) that I almost magically soar from the depths of depression to find myself back on top of the world. These one-off occurrences serve to slingshot me out of the negative headspace in which I might find myself wandering blindly. They do precious little, however, to prevent the inevitable slide back into it, typically incited by the missing of a subsequent target or the return home to all my eagerly awaiting stressors and triggers, where the cycle begins anew.

Without my noticing, the velocity of this cerebral whirlpool has silently increased over the course of the last two years, it's cyclonic reach ever-wider, it's pull ever-stronger. A few weeks ago, without warning, I found myself drowning as I circled the drain of my mind. In a moment of crisis, seeking shelter from the powerful suicidal thoughts which came flooding into my brain, I managed to find the strength to call an emergency line and check myself into the psychiatric ward of a local hospital.

My mental state had deteriorated so gradually over time that, like a frog sitting in a pot of heating water, it didn't occur to me that I was in urgent need of help until it was almost too late. I say that because I should have taken these thoughts far more seriously when they began popping up again. Instead, irresponsibly, naively, I continued to brush them off, chalking them up to little more than a bad attitude, until I found myself trapped in a vortex-like mental state I could no longer pull myself out of.

I want to take this brief moment to implore anyone who finds themselves even brushing with thoughts of suicide to seek professional help immediately. Left unattended, these omens of floundering mental health have the power to increase in strength and severity under a cloak of normalization from which they can spring at any moment to potentially disastrous, irreversible effect. They mustn't be allowed to persist. These thoughts are dangerous, and, in my opinion (as I am by no means a medical professional of any kind, and claim no expertise in this area), must be taken extremely seriously and treated with great urgency. Please, let my experience serve as an example of the dangers of allowing oneself to become desensitized to bouts of suicidal depression.

Thankfully, I am once again receiving the professional help I have clearly needed for far longer than I realized. I am back on the road to a healthy state of mind, and am once again on high alert, noting any signs of my bad mental habits, and forcing myself to work against them.

Finding the Little Yellow Arrows

So, having recognized and admitted that I continue struggling, deeply at times, with some of the very issues I sought to address, having effectively covered the path I repeatedly walk from peak to peak, valley to valley, I ask myself again, what did I actually learn as I marched in-step with thousands of other lost souls, and what did I bring back with me?

Strangely, it's in this exhausting, Sisyphean journey upon which I regularly embark - pushing the boulder up the hill before chasing it back down again - that I find the answer to this question, as well as the hope which has eluded me practically my entire life. While I continue to experience the highs and lows of depression, I know that both the frequency and severity of these depressed states have decreased dramatically over time thanks in no small part to a few precious things which the Camino taught me. Provisioned with ample amounts of time, energy, and space as I trudged across Spain, I managed to drill these lessons into habits and formidable allies in the battle I internally wage against myself.

From the first pages of this journal, the fear in which I live my life makes itself aggressively known. The first entry on Day -6 is dedicated almost entirely to enumerating the endless concerns which plagued me as I prepared myself for the journey ahead. Page after page, I constantly express fears and what-ifs. As soon as I resolve one crop of anxieties, others pop up to take their place. On the Camino and in my life, I play a perpetual game of whack-a-mole with an unquenchable supply of doubts, misgivings, and uncertainties.

Seemingly ignorant to, and unconcerned with, such levels of premeditated worry at the beginning of the trip, well before I even left the Camino I began to recognize the extent to which fear dominates my decision making and erodes the quality of my life. On Day 23, as I walked alone in a misty, wet forest, in one of those rare "Eureka!" moments, I finally understood what President Franklin Delano Roosevelt meant when he famously said, "We have nothing to fear but fear itself." It finally dawned on me how fear corrodes everything it touches, reducing even the most exciting opportunities to little more than a list of potential disappointments and impediments which one must overcome. Ever since, I have continued making conscious efforts to recognize when I'm feeling afraid, ascertain what that fear is attached to, and diminish it by trusting more in myself and my efficacy as a problem solver; in the people around me and their ability to help me when aid is truly needed. I force myself to remain calm in the face of perceived obstacles. I remind myself that the anxieties I project into the future are typically little more than fictional stories my mind has conjured up to cajole me into taking preventative measures against potential failure. Though my battle with fear continues on a daily basis, the more I fight it, the less frequently it taints the exciting opportunities which present themselves; the more I fight being afraid, the more excited I feel to be alive.

En route to Santiago, I began to see that the blanket of fear surrounding my life is inextricably linked to Perfectionism and the merciless punishment I inflict upon myself for any outcome which falls short of my insanely high standards. Crossing vast swathes of open country with nothing but my own company to distract me, I found myself with nowhere to hide from the barrage of attacks my ego leveled against me for any number of inconsequential shortcomings. I paid dearly for minor infractions, like walking a few hundred yards in the wrong direction, or ordering the wrong thing at a restaurant.

Wearied, annoyed, and worn down by this regular onslaught of criticism, I had no recourse but to seek shelter in the tiny neglected buds of forgiveness and self-compassion sprouting in my consciousness. Gradually, and for the first time in my life, I began to comprehend what all of my friends and loved ones meant when they insisted, "Blake, you're far too hard on yourself," and I began to agree with them. As the reality set in that over the last several years I had outright refused to hear them, the pleas of my therapist that I learn to be kind to myself, to treat myself well, to occasionally let myself off the hook began to make sense. I started to see that not only was I not obliged to berate myself, I didn't even deserve that scorn which I so eagerly heaped upon myself. Slowly, I began to offer myself the compassion I so willingly offer to others, and as I treated myself to more forgiveness, an unexpected thing began to happen: the clutches of fear on my psyche began to loosen. Learning that I could approach myself with grace and mercy after some perceived failure greatly diminished the anxiety that potential for failure induced in the first place. In addition, the warm embrace of clemency supported me and lifted me up in moments of weakness, as opposed to the cold shoulder of blame whose abandonment of me in my times of need left me laid out, isolated, and vulnerable to all the bad habits which drag me into despair. In conjunction, self-compassion and a resilience to my own fears create an upward spiral which counteracts the pull of depression.

Buoyed by this positive momentum, I have learned a new technique to overcome the tidal forces of melancholy. Until recently, if I wanted to curb my slide into the abyss, I possessed no other strategy than to fight, struggle, and push against any and all external threats I perceived as prodding me in the wrong direction. Like trying to swim against the current of a powerful river, I constantly burned myself out fighting against forces fully beyond my control. At a certain point, I stopped even distinguishing between good, bad, and neutral influences in my life, and began seeing basically everything in the world around me as a threat. Ironically, by steadfastly resisting everything, I created a pressure-cooker existence which only further oppressed me and hastened my collapse into the void.

But, as I started to learn to show myself compassion, my fears diminished and the perceived threats lessened in both quantity and magnitude. Suddenly, bolstered by this newfound self-love, I found myself able to stand on my own two feet as the waters of uncertainty raged past me. Eventually I could see that I am not doomed to perpetually swim upstream. I could instead choose to just go with the current. It might carry me a ways downstream, but I began to trust that I would eventually be able to swim to shore or grab hold of a passing branch until someone came to my assistance.

Time and again, the Camino forced me to reconsider my habitual rejection of any imperfections in my life. As my left knee throbbed and my frustration mounted, I had no choice but to continually reassess how I chose to approach the issue. I could piss and moan about the pain and the slowed pace, about the injustice and the unfairness, while forcing my body to power through the injury and carry me at my desired pace. This strategy of stubbornness would, at best, only exacerbate the damage already done, and, at worst, force me to quit walking the Camino entirely. Therefore, I was forced to give up the fight altogether. "This is my injured knee. It's not ideal, but it's what I have. I may have to walk slower now, but that's alright. I'll arrive to the albergue just the same. I'll see this as an opportunity to enjoy the scenery, and, more importantly, I'll see this challenge as an opportunity to grow." I had to have that conversation with myself many times throughout the Camino, until eventually it started to bleed into other imperfect moments in my life. Before I knew it, I found myself bending to the pressures of life and finding a way to work with them, rather than destroying myself trying to submit them to my will. The Camino, by putting me at odds with my knee injury, finally helped me understand and harness the power of acceptance.

Combined, these learnings on fear, compassion, and acceptance have helped to relieve an enormous amount of pressure from my daily life and finally allowed me to see that I am enough, I do enough, and I deserve to take some time to enjoy the wonderful things in life. In the past, my fears of inadequacy and that hounding perfectionism herded me from one goal to the next, neither allowing me the time to appreciate nor celebrate anything encountered on the path to reaching them. My time in Finisterre would have almost certainly passed me by unnoticed had it not been for Kyle practically shaking me out of my goal-oriented state, and urging, "Don't forget: enjoy this! [...] We came a long way to get here! Don't forget to feel good about it." He'd be happy to know that I now allow myself far more time and space to rest, relax, and relish my life and the people I have in it. I finally realize that I can and deserve to do so. I've finally awoken to the absurdity of stuffing a life full of adventure, excitement, and fulfilling relationships which I never stop to revel in.

Funnily enough, setting aside the time to contemplate and savour the beautiful things in life makes me more productive, not less, as I've always feared. Unsurprisingly, these moments of respite gladden my spirits and remind me of all the reasons I have to get out of bed and face the day in the first place. They give me the strength to keep hope alive and to continue improving in the face of my demons, rather than giving up and succumbing to them in that final, irreversible act of resignation.

The End of One Camino, the Beginning of Another

David, the hospitalero from Bodenaya, was right when he said, "The true Camino begins after Santiago." The Way itself didn't magically remedy any of the issues I set out hoping to resolve. It did, however, provide me with myriad lessons and ample time for considering how to apply them in order to improve my approach to this precious journey.

Since coming home, I've grappled with what I learned and how I must change if I hope to more thoroughly enjoy life. The answers are not always forthright, but, like the tiny yellow arrows which guided my steps for almost 1000 KM (621.37 mi), I find them here and there, often in unexpected and unusual places.

In a twist of fate I could never have anticipated, the very crests and troughs of my lifelong depression have become beacons I now turn to as symbols of hope. I now see them as reminders that everything is a wave, everything comes and goes in phases. My goal cannot be to eradicate the ups and downs in life. Like trying to simplify the route to Santiago by eradicating the mountains and valleys standing in the way, it would be an act both futile and self-defeating, requiring the destruction of the very things that make the expedition worthwhile; of the Camino itself. Instead, I strive evermore to accept the difficulties which inevitably crop up. Leading with greater trust and compassion for both myself and the world around me I attempt to more effectively navigate life's unavoidable hardships while never losing sight of the fact that the struggles and challenges they present are precisely what make for tales as exciting, beautiful, and human as this one.

I've always known that the way is long, and that the road is difficult. And now, finally, I'm beginning to see that the way is beautiful, and that the road is life.

Buen Camino.

All my lovin',

– Blake.

Let's Keep Walking

Hi there!

I want thank you from the bottom of my heart for taking the time to read my journal and tag along with me on this journey to Santiago.

Although the book is finished, our journey together doesn't have to stop here!

Lost on the Way is full of pictures from my pilgrimage, and you can see all of them in color on my website at www.BlakeFarha.com.

There, you'll also find pictures that weren't included in this book, as well as my blog posts, links for streaming my music, podcasts, YouTube videos, and ways to get in touch with me directly.

And please do get in touch with me. It would be a joy to hear from you.

If you've enjoyed walking The Camino with me, if this journal has brought something positive to your life, whether it be insight, companionship, useful Camino information, or just a few hours of enjoyable reading and daydreaming, it would mean the world to me if you could leave a positive review for *Lost on the Way* on Amazon.com or GoodReads.com.

This will help others find the book, so that it can help and be enjoyed by as many people as possible.

If you're more the analog type, feel free to pass your copy of *Lost on the Way* to someone you think would enjoy it.

Thanks again, and all the best, wherever your Camino takes you from here.

All my lovin',

- Blake.

About the Author

Blake Farha is a voice artist, musician, and performer. Born in Wichita, Kansas in 1986, he grew up in Dallas, Texas where he graduated with a degree in Economics from the University of Texas at Dallas.

Fluent in four-and-a-half languages (his Danish has gotten a bit rusty lately), Blake has spent his adult life hopping from country to country and jumping from career to career.

He currently lives in Berlin where he has devoted himself to his creative pursuits: voice acting, writing and producing music, podcasting, and improv comedy.

Lost on the Way is his first book.

Made in the USA
Las Vegas, NV
24 August 2022

53891921R00194